FOCUS ON TEACHING

For my son Cameron Knight

A computer genius, but more importantly, an incredibly kind-hearted man.
I'm very proud to be your Dad, Cam.

FOCUS ON TEACHING

USING VIDEO
FOR HIGH-IMPACT INSTRUCTION

JIM KNIGHT

CORWIN
A SAGE Company

learningforward

A JOINT PUBLICATION

CORWIN
A SAGE Company

For information:

Corwin

A SAGE Company

2455 Teller Road

Thousand Oaks, California 91320

(800) 233-9936

www.corwin.com

SAGE Publications Ltd.

1 Oliver's Yard

55 City Road

London EC1Y 1SP

United Kingdom

SAGE Publications India Pvt. Ltd.

B 1/I 1 Mohan Cooperative Industrial Area

Mathura Road, New Delhi 110 044

India

SAGE Publications Asia-Pacific Pte. Ltd.

3 Church Street

#10-04 Samsung Hub

Singapore 049483

Acquisitions Editor: Dan Alpert

Associate Editor: Kimberly Greenberg

Editorial Assistant: Cesar Reyes

Production Editor: Melanie Birdsall

Copy Editor: Kim Husband

Typesetter: C&M Digitals (P) Ltd.

Proofreader: Caryne Brown

Indexer: Sheila Bodell

Graphic Designer: Gail Buschman

Cover design by Clinton Carlson.

Printed in the United States of America

Library of Congress Cataloging-in-Publication Data

A catalog record of this book is available from the Library of Congress.

ISBN: 978-1-4833-4412-6

This book is printed on acid-free paper.

SUSTAINABLE FORESTRY INITIATIVE

Certified Chain of Custody
Promoting Sustainable Forestry
www.sfiprogram.org
SFI-01268

SFI label applies to text stock

14 15 16 17 18 10 9 8 7 6 5 4 3 2 1

CONTENTS

LIST OF COMPANION WEBSITE RESOURCES

 Access the following videos and resources at
www.corwin.com/focusonteaching

PREFACE

I learned about the power of video from my friend and colleague Mike Hock close to two decades ago when we were both doctoral students at the University of Kansas. Mike had created a successful tutoring program, Strategic Tutoring (Hock, Schumaker, & Deshler, 2001), and he spent a fair amount of time training tutors to tutor in a way that ensured students learned how to learn as they completed academic tasks.

In his work with tutors, Mike noticed that many were struggling to learn and fluently implement the specific stages and practices that made up strategic tutoring. He decided to video-record the tutors in action and then have them watch themselves tutoring and analyze their practices with the help of a checklist. The results were amazing! When tutors saw themselves on video, they quickly realized how they needed to improve, and their tutoring significantly improved.

I could see that video was a powerful learning tool for educators, but video was such a hassle at the time. We had to get cameras—they were usually expensive—set them up, tape a session, and then transfer the video to a VHS tape so we could watch it. Besides, the rather large camera on a tripod usually disrupted the class so that whenever we brought a camera into a teacher's classroom, the class inevitably ended up being largely about the camera. In other words, even though video clearly worked, it took too much effort and caused too many distractions.

In 2006, I got a solution for the video hassle from an unlikely source: Mick Jagger. As I watched the televised coverage of the World Cup that year, I noticed that Mick was shown several times recording the events with a flashy little camera, which I learned was a Flip camera—a tiny, easy-to-use, inexpensive HD camera. Watching Mick film parts of the game, I figured that I could use a Flip camera to record a class without disrupting the teacher's lesson. So I decided to try out Flip cameras as a part of our research at the University of Kansas.

I first introduced cameras to our team of instructional coaches working on our research projects in Topeka, Kansas. We quickly realized that video was a game breaker. Professional learning would never be the same again! As time has passed, technological innovation has made it easier and easier to video-record and share a lesson, and in all likelihood video will become even easier and more powerful as technology advances in the future.

This book summarizes the findings of a number of projects that directly or indirectly studied video and coaching. As mentioned, first, our research team at the Kansas Coaching Project at the University of Kansas and instructional coaches in Topeka, Kansas, explored how video might be integrated into the coaching process. Then our team and instructional coaches from Beaverton, Oregon, employed a design research model (Bradley et al., 2013) to refine how coaches could use video with teachers to gather data on current realities in a classroom, set goals, and monitor progress toward the goals. Our team is now in the midst of a second design study with coaches in Othello, Washington, who are also helping us refine how to use video within the components of coaching.

In addition to these studies, I conducted a study of how to use video or audio recordings to improve communication skills. As part of the research, I received more than 500 reflection reports from people working on their communication skills in countries around the world, including India, Australia, South Korea, the United Kingdom, Canada, and the United States. The volunteer participants in this project, sponsored by the Instructional Coaching Group, wrote about how they used recordings to improve how they listened, built emotional connections, and found common ground during their interactions with others.

Finally, Marilyn Ruggles, my colleague at the Instructional Coaching Group, and I conducted about 50 interviews with teachers, coaches, and principals in U.S. schools about their experiences with video-enhanced professional development. The names and positions of the interviewees, who generously agreed to be interviewed twice, are included in the Acknowledgments.

In writing this book, I have drawn heavily from my interviews and included the comments of teachers, instructional coaches, and principals. All interview comments are taken from transcripts of interviews. In some cases, I have modified comments slightly to increase clarity (e.g., replacing pronouns with antecedents, for example) or made them more concise (e.g., putting two comments together). However, I have been careful to keep the content of each participant's comments intact.

Video changes everything. That is the big message I heard in all of our interviews. But those changes can be helpful or damaging. Used poorly in a compulsory, heavy-handed way, video recording can damage teacher morale at a time when, for many teachers, morale is at an all-time low. Used effectively, in a way that honors teachers' professionalism and learning, video can be the most powerful improvement we have experienced in our schools in a long time. My sincere hope is that this book will enable us to use video effectively in a way that will help us provide the best possible learning opportunities for all of our students.

ACKNOWLEDGMENTS

Let us be grateful to the people who make us happy; they are the charming gardeners who make our souls blossom.

—Marcel Proust

Each publication I write is possible only because of the minds, hearts, and works of many, many people. Educators, authors, researchers, and friends all share ideas with me, and, like potters collectively forming a blob of clay into something useful, we test out ideas and shape our thinking until, I hope, we arrive at something useful. Sometimes I learn from others by reading their books and articles, sometimes I learn by conducting interviews, and sometimes I learn from conversations in classrooms or at kitchen tables. And of the works that I have written, this book is the one that has benefitted the most from help from others.

There is no doubt in my mind that this book would not have been written without the love and support of my family. My wife, Jenny, is my north star, my partner in business and life, my one, true love. She brings tremendous joy into my life, and I am certain I could not have written this book without her love and faith. My parents, Joan and Doug Knight, have always believed in me, and their constant encouragement started me down the research and writing path that I find myself following today. My children, Geoff, Cameron, David, Emily, Ben, Isaiah, and Luke, inspire me, challenge me, and every day more and more increase my optimism about the future because of the good work they do in the world.

I'm grateful to my colleagues at the Instructional Coaching Group, Michelle Harris, Ann Hoffman, Ruth Ryschon, Tricia Skyles, Conn Thomas, and Susan Woodruff. They do an outstanding job organizing and sharing our ideas and they push my thinking when we get the chance to meet and work together. I am also grateful to my research partners at the Kansas Coaching Project at the University of Kansas. My long-time mentors Don Deshler and Jean Schumaker are friends who have taught me as much about life as they have taught me about research and education—and that is an enormous amount. My longtime colleagues Mike Hock, Marti Elford, and Devona Dunekack have worked with me for more than a decade, and I'm grateful for their partnership, for all they do to ensure that our research is successful, and especially for their commitment to children.

Many have contributed a great deal to help make this book a reality. At the Instructional Coaching Group, Marilyn Ruggles conducted most of the interviews that make up a substantial portion of the book; Carol Hatton has taken on numerous tasks to help me find references, create learning maps, edit texts, review notes, and on and on; and our graphic designer Clinton Carlson created the exact cover I wanted even though I didn't know it until I saw it. I also owe a great debt to my copy editor, Kirsten McBride, who has improved just about every page I have written. At Corwin, my indefatigable editor Dan Alpert has stuck with me through thick and thin and encouraged me with warmth and faith, always, when I most needed encouragement. Melanie Birdsall, senior project editor at Corwin, has gracefully and patiently walked this book through the entire production process, while always interacting with patience, kindness, and smarts.

Many educators have contributed significantly to this book by trying out these ideas and sharing what worked and what didn't work. I'm grateful to the coaching teams from Beaverton, Oregon—Susan Leyden, Jennifer MacMillan, and Lea Molczan—and Othello, Washington—Denise Colley, Jared Farley, Marci Gonzalez, Jackie Jewell, and Jenn Perez—who all helped shape what I know about video and instructional coaching. I am also grateful to the many teachers, instructional coaches, and principals who agreed to be interviewed twice, before and after using video-enhanced professional development.

Finally, I'm grateful to the musicians who inspired and energized me as I wrote down word upon word. I began this book listening to the Grateful Dead, especially the Betty Boards from the spring '77 tour. I finished the book listening to the magical jazz created between 1955 and 1960, especially by John Coltrane and Miles Davis. Most days while writing, at some point I found myself listening to Emanuel Ax's wonderful Haydn Piano Sonatas. In my opinion, Ax's Haydn sonatas are the best music to listen to while writing.

Educators Who Graciously Agreed to Implement Video-Enhanced Professional Development and Be Interviewed for This Book and Videos

Jennifer Adams, K–5 Instructional Mathematics Coach, Deerfield Public Schools, Illinois

Crista Anderson, K–12 Title 1 Instructional Coach, Missoula County Public Schools, Montana

Jill Baird, Assistant Principal, Rockwall ISD, Texas

Jean Clark, Special Consultant, Cecil County, Maryland

Sarah Coons, Education Specialist, Wichita Falls, Texas

Amy Grabenkort, Associate Principal, Evergreen Public Schools, Washington

Chad Harnisch, High School Principal, Sauk Prairie School District, Sauk, Wisconsin

Melissa Hickey, Instructional Coach, Capital Region Education Council (CREC), Connecticut

Michael Hodnicki, Instructional Coordinator for Professional Development for Secondary Language Arts and Media, Cecil County Public Schools, Elkton, Maryland

Courtney Horton, Instructional Partner, Madison City Schools, Alabama

Denise Lohmiller, K–5 Elementary District ELAR Coordinator, Rockwall ISD, Texas

Lea Molczan, Sixth-Grade Humanities Teacher, Beaverton School District, Oregon

Tony Mosser, Middle School Science Teacher and Instructional Coach, Spring Lake Park Schools, Minnesota

Kimberly Nguyen, K–4 Special Education Teacher, Delton Kellogg Schools, Michigan

Rychie Rhodes, Clinical Professor, Office of Professional Development, St. Vrain Valley School District, Longmont, Colorado

Catherine Rich, Principal, Phalen Lake Hmong Studies Magnet, St. Paul, Minnesota

Kimberly Richardson, Supervisor of Instruction—Title I, Hampton City Schools, Virginia

Beth Sanders, Secondary Social Studies Connected Educator, Birmingham, Alabama

Caroline Schaab, Instructional Technology Coach, Park Ridge, Illinois

Kirsten Shrout Fernandes, Instructional Coach, The Learning Community Charter School, Central Falls, Rhode Island

Bill Sommers, Middle School Principal, Minnetonka Middle School West, Minnesota

Kandy Streety, Regional Support Staff, Alabama Reading Initiative, Birmingham, Alabama

Sharon Thomas, English Teacher and Instructional Coach, Cecil County Public Schools, Maryland

Amanda Trimble, Instructional Coach 6–8, Noblesville Schools, Indiana

ABOUT THE AUTHOR

 **Jim Knight** is a research associate at the University of Kansas Center for Research on Learning and the president of the Instructional Coaching Group. He has spent close to two decades studying professional learning and instructional coaching. He has written or co-authored several books on the topic, including *Instructional Coaching: A Partnership Approach to Improving Instruction* published by Corwin and Learning Forward (2007), *Unmistakable Impact: A Partnership Approach for Dramatically Improving Instruction* (2011), and *High-Impact Instruction: A Framework for Great Teaching* (2013). Knight co-authored *Coaching Classroom Management* (2006) and edited *Coaching: Approaches and Perspectives* (2008).

Knight has authored articles on instructional coaching and professional learning in publications such as *The Journal of Staff Development, Educational Leadership, Principal Leadership, The School Administrator,* and *Kappan.*

Frequently asked to lead professional learning, Knight has presented and consulted in most states and eight countries. Knight also leads the coaching institutes and the Annual Instructional Coaching Conference in Lawrence, Kansas.

He has a PhD in education from the University of Kansas and has won several university teaching, innovation, and service awards. Knight hosts *Talking About Teaching* on the Teaching Channel and writes the radicallearners.com blog. Contact Knight at jimknight@mac.com.

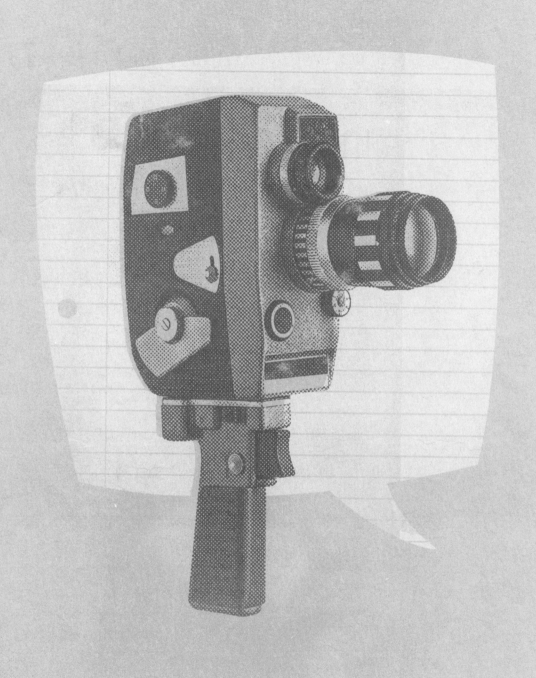

Chapter 1: The Power of Video

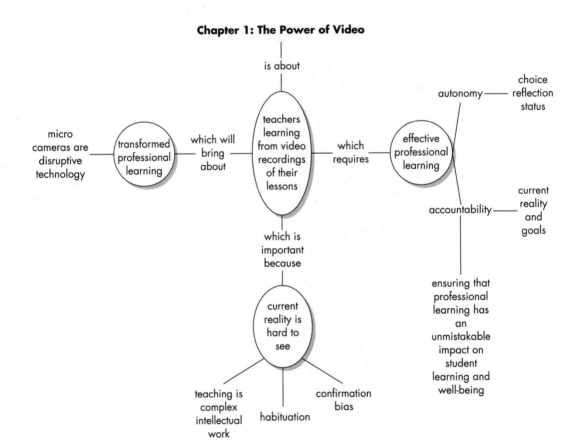

is about

teachers learning from video recordings of their lessons

micro cameras are disruptive technology

transformed professional learning

which will bring about

which requires

effective professional learning

autonomy —— choice reflection status

accountability —— current reality and goals

ensuring that professional learning has an unmistakable impact on student learning and well-being

which is important because

current reality is hard to see

teaching is complex intellectual work

habituation

confirmation bias

1

THE POWER OF VIDEO

Using a video camera during coaching is like opening a door so teachers can observe their own classroom.

—Tara Strahan, Instructional Coach, Orange City, Florida

I learned about the power of video when I watched a video of myself in a research team meeting at the Kansas Coaching Project. We had been asking coaches to record themselves and the teachers they were coaching, so I thought it would only be fair if I watched myself on video. I set up my laptop camera, and during a 45-minute meeting, I recorded my interactions. That night I watched the video recording at home.

Watching myself on video wasn't new to me. I had seen recordings of many of my presentations, but a presentation is tightly structured whereas a meeting is much more spontaneous and dynamic. A meeting makes a bigger demand on your communication skills. Since I taught communication, I was interested in seeing how effectively I interacted with my colleagues, and I was especially interested in this particular meeting because I wanted to find out how I could speak up more since I knew from previous meetings that my colleagues did most of the talking.

I wasn't happy with what I saw. I left the meeting thinking I hadn't had enough time to say what I wanted to say, yet the recording showed that I spoke more than anyone else. And worse, I looked rude. When others were talking, I looked bored. I interrupted people while they were talking. I didn't listen.

While watching the video, I could feel my face getting flushed as I got more and more embarrassed, realizing, "This is what people see all the time when I meet with them!"

It hurt to watch the recording, but that 45-minute video made me want to improve. I realized that I had to change my way of communicating immediately. If I wanted people to collaborate with me, and I did, I had to be the kind of person with whom people would want to collaborate. Video pushed me to change, and video became a way for me to monitor my progress toward being a better collaborator. Such is the power of video.

When we record ourselves doing our work, we see that reality is very different from what we think. As a result, we are often disappointed by what we see. In more than 40 interviews for this book, for example, educators told us again and again that "teachers are way harder on themselves than anyone else would ever dream of being." At other times, we are delighted by what we see, noticing perhaps that a learning activity truly did engage students authentically. Either way, video is a powerful tool for growth and professional learning. As Beth Sanders, a middle school teacher from Birmingham, Alabama, told us, "There is a vulnerability with watching yourself. But I am realizing more and more that my willingness to open the door that video opens up is where growth happens. I really think video is a game changer."

Micro Cameras Are an Example of "Disruptive Technology"

In a flash, new technology can transform the way we do just about anything. Jets revolutionized travel. E-mail altered how we send and get messages. MP3s replaced CDs, which had replaced records. And the Internet has transformed how we do just about everything else, including finding and sharing knowledge, getting help, shopping, meeting people (including significant others), and staying connected.

Micro cameras will be like jet engines for professional learning. Micro cameras such as those built into smartphones, tablets, and other mobile devices are so powerful and easy to use that in just a few years, video-enhanced professional development (VPD) will be a central part of the way teachers learn in most schools around the world.

Micro cameras are an example of what Harvard researcher Clayton M. Christensen (1997) has labeled disruptive technology.

Disruptive technologies usually start out as poor-quality innovations, but over time, as they are improved, they become so powerful and easy to use that they upend entire fields.

Educators have long known that video can be a powerful tool for professional learning, but in the past cameras were too cumbersome, distracting, or of too low a quality to be effective. The increasing quality of video cameras and the promise of ever-more-powerful technologies, coupled with the development of video-sharing websites such as Be a Smarter Cookie, Edthena, Sibme, and the Teaching Channel, means that educators are finding it easier and easier to video-record a lesson and share the recording with colleagues, teams, or students. Professional learning will never be the same.

Why Are Micro Cameras a "Disruptive" Innovation?

Video recording has been a part of teacher education for many decades. In particular, microteaching and National Board Certification have led many teachers to record their lessons and learn from watching the recording. Microteaching was first developed in the early 1960s at Stanford University for teacher education programs. During microteaching, teachers (a) watch a video recording of a master teacher modeling a teaching practice, (b) try out the practice in a brief lesson that was video-recorded, (c) receive feedback from an expert on how they implemented the practice, (d) try out the practice after revising lesson plans, and (e) receive feedback again from experts.

The National Board Certification (http://www.nbpts.org) process has also prompted many teachers to watch themselves teaching on video. The National Board established its teacher program as a response to *A Nation at Risk* (Gardner & Larsen, 1983) to "develop, retain, and recognize accomplished teachers." Today, more than 100,000 teachers are National Board Certified (NBCT), and many others are working toward achieving NBCT status. To be certified, teachers must submit a portfolio of video recordings of teaching practices.

Although the National Board process and microteaching have introduced many teachers to the power of video, the hassle of recording a lesson and watching video has often made it difficult for them to learn all they can learn. Today, those constraints are gone. New, tiny cameras are able to do amazing things that were not possible even 5 years ago. Thus, a micro camera, smaller than a deck of cards, can record high-definition video with reasonably high-quality sound. And with each new generation of a device, the quality of video, the quality of sound, and the ease of use increase at a breakneck pace. Furthermore, the technology we have today is the worst of what we will see in the future. We can only guess at how powerful Google Glass and other new technologies will be as tools for accelerating professional learning. If today's iPhone is my son's Commodore 64, as Jaime Casap from Google has said, just imagine what type of technology will be available in 5, 10, or 20 years.

Video-recording a class used to involve signing out an expensive camera from the principal's office or the AV department, setting it up on a tripod, figuring out how to follow the complicated manual for how to operate the camera, and then converting the recording to a medium that could be viewed on a TV screen. There was nothing discreet about a big camera set up on a tripod in a teacher's classroom. Recording a lesson took a lot of work, usually upset classroom routines and distracted students, and then only produced low-quality video. All of that has changed!

Now a teacher can set up her iPad in her class in about 5 seconds and get a reasonably high-quality video of exactly what happens during a lesson. Setting up a camera is quick, doesn't disrupt the class, and involves pushing one button. Then at the end of the day, the teacher can look over her lesson to either set a new goal or monitor her progress toward a goal that she has already set. Additionally, in order to move closer to her goal, she can implement high-yield instructional practices, such as those described in *High-Impact Instruction: A Framework for Great Teaching* (Knight, 2013), which I will refer to throughout this book, or other books such Marzano's (2007) *The Art and Science of Teaching*, Saphier, Haley-Speca, and Gower's (2008) *Skillful Teacher*, or Lemov's (2010) *Teach Like a Champion*. Video has enormous potential for improving teaching and learning.

> *Using a video camera to learn about your teaching is like looking into a mirror. You get to actually see what you are doing and all of your actions. You are able to see what you normally couldn't see with your own set of eyes.*
>
> —**Courtney Horton**, Instructional Coach, Madison, Alabama

Why Video Is Important

Perhaps the major reason video is so useful for learning is that it helps us see exactly what it looks like when we teach or our students learn. This is important because professionals often do not have a clear picture of what it looks like when they do their work. In our research conversations, teachers and coaches tell us that when they see video recordings of their lessons, they are often amazed at what the video reveals. Many times, teachers are pleased to see evidence that their lessons are working. In other cases, teachers are disappointed (every coach told us that teachers tend to be extremely hard on themselves) by what they see.

Sometimes teachers are both pleased and disappointed. Kimberly Nguyen, a teacher in Michigan, watched two classes she was teaching, her most and her least engaged. She was surprised to see that she was a different teacher in each room. During our interview, Kim said,

> What I really noticed was that with the engaged group, I am much more animated, and I interact more. With the second group, I really struggle with my mood, and my response time is lower. In that class, I think, I am really boring.

Many people, we have learned, have had the same experience as Kimberly: They do not know what it looks like when they teach until they see the video. And because they are unaware of what it looks like when they teach, they often do not feel the need to change. They might be open to trying new practices, but they don't feel compelled to change.

James Prochaska, John Norcross, and Carlo DiClemente's (1994) research into the personal experience of change provides us with language for describing and understanding why people are so surprised by what they see in video recordings. After conducting more than 55 clinical studies of change with more than 1,000 people, Prochaska and his colleagues concluded that the first stage of change is what he refers to as precontemplation. Change begins with people "pre" "contemplating" change; that is, at the start, people aren't even thinking they want to change. Prochaska writes, "G. K. Chesterton might have been describing precontemplators when he said, 'It isn't that they can't see the solution. It is that they can't see the problem'" (p. 40).

Our work with teachers, coaches, and principals has led us to similar conclusions. When we show videos of lessons to teachers, their response is often that they had no idea that their class looked the

> *When you are in the middle of teaching, you just don't see so many things. I had a teacher who was very surprised because she saw students being kind to each other on the other side of the room, and she noticed them helping and sharing. You don't see that when you are going around in small groups. That aspect of video is really nice. You also see areas where you could provide more support. It is the outliers that you just don't catch when you are teaching.*
>
> —**Tara Strahan**, Instructional Coach, Orange City, Florida

way it looked on video. To Beth Sanders, a teacher in Alabama, watching video puts her inside the situation of her class:

> It is much different being in the situation vs. being outside the situation looking in. It is really important to me that I am kind of getting the full-circle view of my classroom, seeing things that matter, things that could be better, and things that I can do to hopefully make things better by watching my class.

Watching yourself on video feels similar to the often unsettling experience of hearing a recording of your voice for the first time—but to the power of 10.

There are many reasons people are precontemplative and have such little awareness of what it looks like when they do the work that they do. Three main reasons are the busyness of teaching, habituation, and confirmation bias.

The Busyness of Teaching. Anyone who spends even a short period of time in a classroom quickly realizes one big reason many teachers have an incomplete understanding of everything that occurs in their classroom: Teachers have too much to think about while teaching to also be able to step back and oversee everything that is happening in their classes.

The authors of *Introduction to Teaching: Becoming a Professional* contend that "teachers make somewhere between 800 and 1,500 decisions every day" (Kauchak & Eggen, 2005, p. 55). For example, teachers must think about delivering material, monitoring student learning and behavior, setting up activities, and maintaining engagement, all while keeping an eye on the clock. As a result, for most, it is extremely difficult to step back and take in everything that is happening in the class while teaching.

Habituation. A second reason many professionals struggle to get a clear picture of reality in the classroom stems from a phenomenon psychologists refer to as habituation—the fact that we lose our sensitivity to just about anything we experience repeatedly. Through habituation, therefore, we can become desensitized to any experience, pleasant or unpleasant, beautiful or ugly. This means that what at one time would have been impossible not to see can eventually become practically invisible.

When habituation happens in the classroom, it can have dire consequences. First, teachers can forget about the true joy of this work, how important and beautiful it is to teach—to empower students to read and write, to become numerate, to help them transcend their social status, to mentor them to be the first in their family to go to college, and much more. Second, teachers can stop seeing children when they aren't learning. They can stop noticing students who are bored, wasting time, or hating school. They can come to believe that off-task behavior and poor performance are all that can be expected from students.

Confirmation Bias. A third reason we may not get a clear picture of reality in the classroom is confirmation bias. In *Decisive*, Heath and Heath (2013) describe confirmation bias as our natural tendency to seek data that support our assumptions:

> Our normal habit in life is to develop a quick belief about a situation and then seek out information that bolsters our belief . . . Researchers have found this result again and again. When people have the opportunity to collect information from the world, they are more likely to select information that supports their preexisting attitudes, beliefs, and actions. (p. 11)

This tendency to seek out support for our beliefs can keep us from getting a clear picture of reality. Thus, for example, we might take the correct answers of four students as evidence that all students are learning, or we might take a student's failure to learn as evidence that he lacks motivation rather than as a prompt to change our teaching.

Our tendency to seek out data that confirm our biases is further increased by the anxiety we feel when we realize students are not learning and we don't know what to do. In such cases, we may be especially inclined to find proof that we are not at fault.

> *Using a video camera to watch your teaching is like having the ability to go back in time because it allows you to take something that has already happened and really look at it, think about it, and see what you would want to change.*
>
> **—Kimberly Nguyen**,
> Teacher, Delton, Michigan

The power of video is that it cuts through habituation, confirmation bias, and the complexity of teaching and shows a true picture of what is happening. Tennis coach Timothy Gallwey (1974) tells a story about the power of getting a clear picture of reality in his book *The Inner Game of Tennis*. Gallwey writes about working with Jack, who "considered his erratic backhand one of the major problems of his life." Jack knew that he took his racket back too high on his backswing because "at least five different pros told [him] so." After watching Jack take a few practice swings, Gallwey concluded that "the five pros were right." Yet despite all the advice, Jack hadn't changed his swing.

Gallwey asked Jack to stand in front of a large reflective window and watch his swing:

> We walked over to a large windowpane and there I asked him to swing again while watching his reflection. He did so, again taking his characteristic hitch at the back of his swing, but this time he was astounded. "Hey, I really do take my racket back high! It goes up above my shoulder!" . . .
>
> What surprised me was Jack's surprise. Hadn't he said that five pros had told him his racket was too high? I was certain that if I had told him the same thing after his first swing, he would have replied, "Yes, I know." But what was now clear was that he didn't *really* know, since no one is ever surprised at seeing something they already know. Despite all those lessons, he had never *directly* experienced his racket going back high.
>
> At the end of the day, Jack said by watching himself in the window, he'd "learned more in ten minutes . . . than in twenty hours of lessons I've taken on my backhand." (pp. 22–24)[1]

Such is the power of seeing yourself doing what you do! Video recordings give us a chance to see, as tennis player Jack did, what it really looks like when we do what we do. Video provides a clear picture of reality, which is critical for setting meaningful goals and monitoring progress toward those goals. But video is most powerful when it is a part of professional learning that is designed to have maximum impact, such as the professional learning approach I describe in *Unmistakable Impact: A Partnership Approach to Dramatically Improving Instruction* (Knight, 2011). VPD will not have any impact unless it is part of an overall approach to learning that focuses on meaningful goals and celebrates the professionalism of teachers.

Accountability *and* Autonomy

When describing professional learning, people often adopt an either/ or stance. For example, some believe that instructional leaders must

---

[1]I'm grateful to Bob Tschannen-Moran, co-author of *Evocative Coaching: Transforming Our Schools One Conversation at a Time* (Tschannen-Moran & Tschannen-Moran, 2010), for first sharing this story with me.

hold teachers accountable in order to improve the way they teach. If there's no accountability, they claim, no meaningful improvement will happen in classrooms. Others say the exact opposite: Because they are professionals, teachers must have complete control over their learning. The idea that teachers would be "held accountable," they say, is insulting to the profession of teachers.

After collaborating with schools around the world for a decade and a half, I have come to believe that professional learning is not either one or the other—both are needed. That is, effective professional development honors the autonomy of teachers but recognizes the importance of a form of accountability grounded in that autonomy. Both are essential.

WHAT DO WE MEAN BY AUTONOMY?

Autonomy, as I've written about in *Unmistakable Impact: A Partnership Approach for Dramatically Improving Instruction* (Knight, 2011), involves at least three elements: choice, thinking, and status. Each of these is briefly described below.

Choice. At its heart, autonomy involves offering choices—in this context, trusting professionals to make many of their own decisions. If we don't allow others some measure of choice, any change initiative is doomed to fail. The surest way to ensure that people won't do something, whether they are 6 or 66 years old, is to tell them they have to do it. In Timothy Gallwey's (1974) words, "When you insist, they will resist."

Giving people choices is important for other reasons than just reducing resistance. If we tell staff they must do what we, the principal, the central office, or the state, say they must do, we are working from the assumption that there is only one answer and that we know what it is, or at least that we know better than they what they should do.

In reality, however, those who work directly with students know a lot about what is best for those students. Teachers' knowledge should be embraced, not suppressed. When we give teachers choices, we ask them to think carefully about what they are implementing in light of what they know rather than simply implementing a one-size-fits-all plan. And when teachers' knowledge is a part of the process of planning and implementing, better teaching occurs.

Finally, choice is important because when we employ professional development programs that don't give teachers choices, we are, in effect, pushing an approach that can only be called dehumanizing. As

Freire (1970) states, "freedom . . . is the indispensable condition for the quest for human completion . . . without freedom [we] cannot exist authentically" (p. 31). Similarly, Peter Block (1993) emphasizes the primacy of choice: "Partners each have a right to say no. Saying no is the fundamental way we have of differentiating ourselves. To take away my right to say no is to claim sovereignty over me . . . If we cannot say no, then saying yes has no meaning" (pp. 30–31).

Thinking. If we want reflective educators, teachers who think, we must make sure that teachers are free to make meaningful decisions about what and how they teach. Telling people exactly what they must do leaves no room for thinking. Autonomy, therefore, is also essential for reflective practice. Thomas Davenport (2005) describes the attributes of people who use their knowledge, skills, and imagination to do their work—knowledge workers—in his book *Thinking for a Living: How to Get Better Performance and Results From Knowledge Workers*. Based on interviews and surveys designed to identify the attributes of knowledge workers, Davenport found that "one important characteristic of knowledge workers" is their need for autonomy:

> Knowledge workers . . . don't like to be told what to do. Thinking for a living engenders thinking for oneself. Knowledge workers are paid for their education, experience, and expertise, so it is not surprising that they take offense when someone else rides roughshod over their intellectual territory. (p. 15)

A teacher with 32 children, who is trying to communicate clearly, to keep each student engaged, and to gauge how well each student is learning, is a prime example of a such a professional.

In *Unmistakable Impact* (Knight, 2011), influenced by Donald Schön (1991) and Joellen Killion (Killion & Todnem, 1991), I divide reflection into three processes: "looking back," "looking at," and "looking ahead." The ability to think for yourself, autonomy, is essential for each, and each way of reflecting is an important part of how teachers learn from video-recording their lessons.

When we "look back," we consider an event that has passed and think about how it proceeded and what we might have done differently. When teachers use video recordings to "look back" at a lesson, they explore what worked and what didn't work and reflect on what they might do differently in the future. Schön refers to this as "reflection on action."

When we "look at," we are thinking about what we are doing in the midst of the act itself. For this form of reflection, therefore, teachers think about their actions based on what they learned from watching a video of a previous lesson. Teachers often see their classes through new eyes after watching their lessons and therefore might make adjustments based on that insight—increasing praise, adjusting activities to increase student motivation, clarifying expectations, and so forth. Schön refers to this way of thinking as "reflection in action."

Finally, "looking ahead" is thinking about how to use an idea, practice, or plan in the future. When we "look ahead," we consider something we have to do in the future and what we can do to ensure success. Teachers collaborating with instructional coaches, for example, might "look ahead" by using a video recording as a point of departure for exploring how ideas might be adapted to meet the needs of students in a future lesson. Killion and Todnem (1991) refer to this as "reflection for practice."

Whether "looking back," "looking at," or "looking ahead," teachers are quintessential knowledge workers, and if they are going to use video effectively, they need autonomy since autonomy is essential for reflection. Most of us want our children to be taught by reflective professionals who think for themselves rather than by skilled laborers who primarily implement what they are trained to do. To get the kind of teachers we want for our children, we must ensure teachers have the autonomy they need to truly be reflective practitioners.

Status. A final reason autonomy is important is that denying autonomy sets up an unequal relationship that interferes with learning among professionals. That is, when teachers don't have autonomy, those who tell them what to do clearly have more power. Edgar Schein (2009) makes this case in his book *Helping: How to Offer, Give, and Receive Help*:

> All human relationships are about status positioning and what sociologists call "situational proprieties." It is human to want to be granted the status and position that we feel we deserve, no matter how high or low it might be, and we want to do what is situationally appropriate. We are either trying to get ahead or stay even, and we measure all interactions by how much we have lost or gained. (p. xi)

According to Schein (2009), we do not feel a conversation has been successful unless we are given the status we think we deserve.

> When a conversation has not been equitable we sometimes feel offended. That usually means that the value we have claimed for ourselves has not been acknowledged, or that the other person or persons did not realize who we were or how important our communication was. (p. 30)

Like anyone else, teachers disengage from conversations, as Schein suggests, when they perceive they are not getting the status they deserve. And being prescriptive with teachers in ways that deny choice and reflection inevitably puts them in a one-down position. When people feel one-down, they are "vulnerable to dysfunctional, defensive behavior" (Schein, 2009, p. 37). Additionally, according to Schein, "if the other person acts very parental by talking down to us, we may feel it is appropriate to act childish by being passive aggressive" (p. 25).

In other words, teachers who make it clear that they are not listening during a workshop by reading newspapers, grading, or engaging in side conversations are communicating that they refuse to be put in a one-down position. Put differently, doing sudoku, rather than listening in a workshop, is a way of saying, "I'm not going to put you in a one-up position." Giving teachers meaningful autonomy is one way by which leaders can give teachers the status they deserve and, in the process, dramatically decrease "dysfunctional, defensive behavior" (Knight, 2009).

In short, autonomy is a vital part of authentic professional learning that makes an impact. When we do not give teachers autonomy, we deprofessionalize teaching by suppressing teacher knowledge and humanity, inhibit reflection, and dramatically increase the likelihood of resistance. Positioning teachers as equal partners—see *Instructional Coaching: A Partnership Approach to Improving Instruction* (Knight, 2007) and *Unmistakable Impact* (Knight, 2011) for more information on how to do that—is essential. However, autonomy will not bring about the changes we need to see in schools without accountability.

WHAT IS ACCOUNTABILITY?

When the term *accountability* is used in professional learning, it has many different meanings. For example, it may mean that teachers have to give an account of what they do and implement a program or practice that others have chosen for them. Accountability also might mean that teachers are accountable to district leaders, students, or parents. However it is described, accountability means to be obligated to act in certain ways for reasons that are external to us.

How is it possible, then, for teachers to be both accountable and autonomous? For our purposes here, when educators are accountable, their professional learning has an unmistakable impact on student learning. In this way, educators are accountable to the process, and especially to children, parents, other stakeholders, and the profession of teaching. Furthermore, at the individual or school level, accountability is a genuine commitment to learning and growth on the part of every educator, a recognition that to have learning students, we need learning teachers, learning coaches, and learning administrators.

Some insight into how this kind of accountability can coexist with autonomy can be gained by reviewing Robert Fritz's work. More than three decades ago, Fritz (1984) described the dynamics of personal growth in his book *The Path of Least Resistance*. Growth, he wrote, involves two factors: a clear picture of current reality and a clear goal. When we know our current reality and commit to an improvement goal, we create a tension that compels us to strive to get better so long as we remain committed to the goal. Peter Senge (2006) summarized Fritz's ideas as follows:

> The juxtaposition of vision (what we want) and a clear picture of current reality (where we are relative to what we want) generates what we call creative tension: a force to bring them together, caused by the natural tendency of tension to seek resolution. The essence of personal mastery is learning how to generate and sustain creative tension in our lives. (p. 132)

Two factors, then, are essential for growth as described by Fritz and Senge: a clear picture of reality and a clear goal. These two factors are also essential for accountability as I describe it here. Meaningful change will not happen in a classroom or school unless both of those factors are in place. If there is no picture of reality, we cannot be sure that whatever professional learning is taking place addresses what is most needed. Additionally, if there is no goal, we are unable to monitor progress and determine success. Professional learning that is not grounded in current reality and not focused on a goal will most likely not produce significant change.

Let's look at how this might work for an individual teacher. Imagine a teacher who views a recording of her lesson and realizes that only 5 of her 31 students are answering the questions she is asking. After watching the video, she might set a goal of 20 of her students responding to questions during each lesson. Then, once she has set the goal, she can try various strategies to meet her goal. For example, she might use Thinking Prompts, Effective Questions, or a cooperative learning structure such as Think, Pair, Share from *High-Impact Instruction* (Knight, 2013) or other resources on effective instruction. She could use her camera to monitor her progress toward the goal. As long as she remains committed to her goal, she can keep trying strategies or refining what she is implementing until she hits her goal.

This is an example of professional learning that is accountable—measurable changes will occur that will mean real improvements for students. However, this type of professional learning also involves a high degree of autonomy because the teacher observes her own lesson, sets her own goal, monitors progress, and determines when she has hit the goal.

In the rest of this book, we will see how VPD can be structured to respect the autonomy of professional teachers and at the same time hold them accountable so as to lead to unmistakable improvements in learning. We will see autonomous and accountable professional learning for individual teachers learning alone, with coaches, with teams, or with administrators.

Specifically, the book includes the following features:

Each chapter begins with a learning map depicting the key concepts in the chapter. Each chapter also contains these features:

- **Turning Ideas Into Action**, suggestions for how students, teachers, coaches, and principals can use chapter ideas to improve instruction
- A summary of the chapter under the heading **To Sum Up**
- A **Going Deeper** section that introduces resources readers can explore to extend their knowledge of the ideas and strategies discussed
- **QR codes** with links to videos of teachers, instructional coaches, and administrators describing how they use video recordings to support professional learning in their schools

Finally, throughout the book you will find numerous checklists clarifying how video recording can be used by teachers, coaches, teams, and principals.

The following is a brief description of the contents of the remaining chapters.

Chapter 2: Getting Started With Video-Enhanced Professional Development provides important nuts-and-bolts information about making video recording a part of professional learning. Specifically, the chapter includes suggestions for what kind of camera to use, where to place the camera, and how to share video. Additionally, the chapter describes important considerations such as what kind of consent is required for recording video, when (if ever) to share video, and what issues to address with respect to video-recording students. Finally, the chapter discusses six errors leaders must avoid if they want video recording to be successfully used in their schools.

Chapter 3: Instructional Coaches describes how instructional coaches can use micro cameras to accelerate the coaching process, including for getting a clear picture of what is happening in a classroom, setting goals with teachers, monitoring progress, and serving as a third point for dialogue around instruction. The chapter also makes suggestions for how coaches can enroll teachers in the use of video, explains why video should initially be watched separately by coaches and teachers, and identifies what coaches can do to facilitate dialogue with teachers.

Chapter 4: Teachers Using Cameras to Coach Themselves describes how teachers can coach themselves through the use of video. Specifically, the chapter explores why teachers should watch video of their classes at least twice, when teachers should focus on their students vs. their own instruction, data points that teachers can attend to while watching recordings to get a clearer understanding of what is occurring in their classes, how to set measurable goals for improvement, and how to monitor progress toward those goals.

Chapter 5: Video Learning Teams (VLTs) describes how teams of teachers can come together to share video of their lessons and learn from each other. Specifically, the chapter discusses what principals or instructional coaches should do to create a trusting learning culture for a team, why teams should be voluntary rather than compulsory, and how teams can establish authentic team norms and present activities team members can use to facilitate team learning, such as watching many different examples of teachers implementing practices, focusing on specific practices (such as "I do it, we do it, you do it") or ratio of interactions.

Chapter 6: Principals describes the essential role that principals play in leading the use of video as a part of professional learning in schools. Specifically, the chapter reviews how principals can best support instructional coaches, guide teachers toward self-coaching, and lead or support VLTs. Additionally, the chapter describes how principals can use video to ensure that the teacher evaluation process is a useful, constructive part of teacher professional learning.

Turning Ideas Into Action

STUDENTS

Our schools are successful only if our children are successful. Ultimately, therefore, all professional learning should be judged by the standard of student success. For that reason, students should be among the first people asked about the success or failure of teaching practices. As I explain in *High-Impact Instruction* (Knight, 2013), students can be involved in the conversation about their learning and provide extremely helpful insight into the effectiveness of our teaching. In some cases, students can even be involved in discussing instruction, and volunteer students can be asked to watch video of lessons and subsequently comment on what helps and hinders their learning. This won't work for every student, but at a minimum students can be asked for feedback on what learning activities increase their engagement, make them feel psychologically safe, and inspire them to strive to be better.

TEACHERS

Video is not for everyone. Some teachers simply find it too difficult to watch themselves on video, but for teachers who use it, video offers great opportunities for great learning. Teachers who record their classes will be able to use the recordings to get a clear picture of reality, to set goals, and to monitor progress toward those goals until meaningful change that helps students has occurred.

COACHES

Instructional coaches can use video recordings during all components of coaching. Like teachers who self-coach, instructional coaches can video-record teachers to get a clear picture of reality, to set goals, and to monitor progress toward those goals until meaningful change that helps students has occurred. Further, video recordings can be used as the point of departure for most coaching conversations.

PRINCIPALS

If principals want teachers to use video to improve their teaching methods, principals should use video to improve their own practices. For example, principals can record the way they facilitate meetings to identify ways in which they can be clearer, more efficient, and more supportive. Additionally, principals can walk the talk by recording themselves teaching, sharing the video during a staff meeting, and then allowing themselves to be coached by the instructional coach during the meeting. When a principal walks the talk in such a way, he or she will likely find that many more teachers agree to do video recording of their lessons.

SYSTEM LEADERS AND POLICY MAKERS

All of the teachers interviewed for this book acknowledged that although they thought video was incredibly helpful, lack of time was a major barrier to VPD. Kimberly Nguyen's comments are typical:

> I think the problem with implementing it with any real success would be time—time for someone to video themselves, and sit down and look at it, and analyze it. It helps if you have a coach, but you really have to be committed to do it by yourself.

For this reason, leaders who want teachers to use video must build in time for them to do this important work. Time might come from early-release days for students or additional payment for teachers who are willing to put in time (either by themselves or with a coach) to record a class, set a goal, and make the changes necessary to hit the goal. When time is structured into teachers' days so that they can do this powerful reflective learning, they will be able to make significant, meaningful improvements in the way their students learn. Without time, it's likely that little significant change will occur.

TO SUM UP

- Video is a disruptive technology that will transform the way professional learning occurs in schools.
- Video is essential because professionals don't have a clear picture of what they do when they do their work.

- Teachers struggle to get a clear picture of reality because of the demands of teaching, habituation, and confirmation bias.
- Effective professional learning involves accountability that respects, even celebrates, teacher autonomy.
- Autonomy involves choice, thinking, and status.
- Accountability as defined here involves establishing clear, measurable goals and then working to implement them.
- Accountability means ensuring that learning has an unmistakable, positive impact on student learning and well-being.
- Both accountability and autonomy are essential for effective professional learning.

GOING DEEPER

Clayton Christensen's (1997) *The Innovator's Dilemma: The Revolutionary Book That Will Change the Way You Do Business* is the classic work on how disruptive technology transforms business. *Disrupting Class: How Disruptive Innovation Will Change the Way the World Learns*, co-authored by Christensen, Curtis W. Johnson, and Michael B. Horn (2008), applies Christensen's theory to innovation in education.

Heath and Heath's (2013) *Decisive: How to Make Better Choices in Life and Work* explains how confirmation bias and three other biases can dramatically interfere with our ability to make decisions and offers excellent suggestions for how to overcome those biases and, as a result, make sound decisions about the most important issues in our lives.

Richard Tedlow's (2010) *Denial: Why Business Leaders Fail to Look Facts in the Face—and What to Do About It* is a business book that also has implications for educators. Tedlow's main point is that most of us deny reality, and unless we learn to confront reality, our personal and organizational work will suffer.

Finally, in many ways, this book is an extension of my earlier works. For example, in *Unmistakable Impact: A Partnership Approach to Dramatically Improving Instruction* (Knight, 2011), I describe the necessity of positioning teachers as professionals and explain why dehumanizing professional education (that thwarts teacher autonomy) is unlikely to succeed. In *High-Impact Instruction: A Framework for Great Teaching* (Knight, 2013), I present practices that teachers can use to improve their instruction after watching video and setting goals.

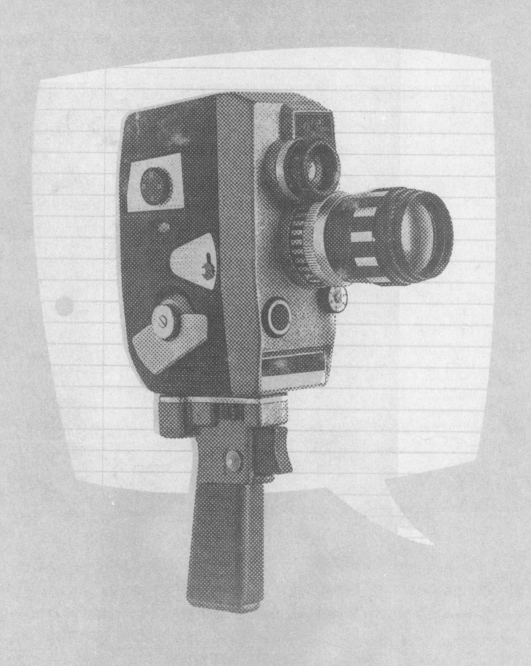

**Chapter 2: Getting Started With
Video-Enhanced Professional Development**

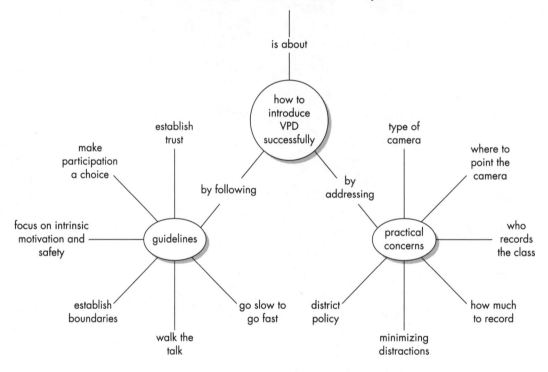

2

GETTING STARTED WITH VIDEO-ENHANCED PROFESSIONAL DEVELOPMENT

Using a video camera to learn about your teaching is like childbirth. You have a lot of anxiety going into it, and it's painful while you are going through it, but if you see it through to the end, you will end up having a much better result than you ever could have imagined.

—Sharon Thomas, High School English Teacher,
Cecil County, Maryland

Lea Molzcan is a middle school reading teacher from Beaverton, Oregon. Lea is one of four instructional coaches we partnered with when my colleagues and I at the Kansas Coaching Project studied instructional coaching and, eventually, video cameras. Lea is a masterful coach and teacher. As a coach, she made her collaborating teachers feel safe and empowered. When we watched video of Lea asking questions and listening during our focus group meetings at the University of Kansas, everybody—coaches and researchers— wanted to be more like Lea.

One of the goals of the study in which Lea participated was to find out how cameras could be used most successfully during instructional coaching. At the start of our team's first meeting,

I handed everyone a shiny new Flip camera and asked them to try it out by recording a partner, being recorded by a partner, and then watching the video by themselves. I thought this would be a simple way for the coaches to ensure they knew how to use the camera.

Everyone gladly did the recording, but when they watched the video recordings of themselves, the mood in the room immediately changed. Lea's reaction to seeing herself was especially powerful. Overcome with emotion, she broke into tears. "I cried," Lea said. "I was really upset with the way I looked."

I remember watching Lea during that session and wondering whether I was asking too much of people by suggesting that they record and watch themselves. However, Lea and her fellow coaches from Beaverton, Michelle Harris, Jennifer MacMillan, and Susan Leyden, ultimately convinced me that video can be an incredibly powerful tool for learning. Indeed, after 3 years studying their coaching procedures, the coaches agreed that watching video was the single most important part of their professional learning. Lea, back teaching again, now considers video an essential part of her development:

> I think I've gotten so used to being taped that it doesn't bother me to record myself. It is natural for me to have the camera on. It has become old hat for me.
>
> Video is a great tool and so easy to use. You can do it quickly and on the fly. There is not a lot of planning involved. You can do it for a short time or a long time. You have complete control. I will absolutely keep using it.

At first, most people are not particularly excited about watching themselves on video, so it takes a little time to get used to it. For example, high school English teacher Sharon Thomas said, "I think there is this disparity between the way we feel when we are in front of the classroom and what it looks like to a normal person. When I teach, I am so comfortable up there. I'm Audrey Hepburn. I'm Gwyneth Paltrow. I love it so much. Then I see the video and think, 'Who is that middle-aged lady up there?'"

But when you get used to watching yourself, used to your voice, the way you look, and your surprising vocalizations, you can learn a lot. "People are terrified at first," instructional coach Courtney Horton noted, adding,

> [B]ut video is an excellent way to learn with teachers. So often we don't even know how we teach or what we do. Video is a great tool to catch things you might not even know about.

Watching a video of your lesson is like watching yourself in a mirror, but you are able to see what you normally wouldn't see with just your own set of eyes.

Sharon Thomas, and indeed everyone we interviewed, emphasized the importance of working through the awkwardness of watching yourself on video. "Give yourself time to get used to seeing and hearing yourself on the video recording. It's OK to be horrified the first few times. But stick with it. Video really is the thing that is going to help you move forward. How good we are with kids, how well we are serving kids, how much we care about our profession . . . this is all a really big deal."

Video 2.1
An Overview of How Video Can Be Used

www.corwin.com/ focusonteaching

Getting Started

Since video has such great potential for accelerating growth, the temptation might be to rush to get VPD up and flying in every classroom in every school right away. However, given the complex emotional reactions to watching a video of oneself, leaders must take the time necessary to set up VPD in such a way that it has an excellent chance to succeed. In fact, if VPD is not implemented with care, it can interfere with, rather than improve, professional learning.

To increase the likelihood that VPD will succeed, educators should follow a few guidelines for success and address a few practical concerns. Each of these is addressed in this chapter.

Guidelines for Success

Cameras can be extremely useful for enhancing professional practice, but if cameras are used in a way that diminishes teachers' professionalism, they will be good for neither students nor teachers. To increase the chances that VPD will be embraced, educators should keep in mind a few simple guidelines when introducing video in their schools.

> **Guidelines for Introducing Video**
>
> 1. Establish trust.
> 2. Make participation a choice.
> 3. Focus on intrinsic motivation and safety.
> 4. Establish boundaries.
> 5. Walk the talk.
> 6. Go slow to go fast.

1. ESTABLISH TRUST

One of the most frequent questions I hear about video is, "How do you get teachers to do it?" When I asked that question of the coaches in our study, who had each collaborated with teachers who agreed to watch themselves on video multiple times, their first answer wasn't very helpful. They said, "I just asked them, and they said yes." Then I asked them why their teachers agreed, and now their answers were very helpful. "They worked with us," the coaches said, "because they trusted us. So if teachers are not agreeing to be video-recorded, maybe the issue isn't the video; maybe the issue is trust."

Many have written about the role of trust within professional learning. Amy Edmondson, the Novartis Professor of Leadership and Management at Harvard University, who has dedicated much of her academic life to studying how people work and learn together, concludes that people need to feel psychologically safe in order to be productive and learn. "In corporations, hospitals, and government agencies," Edmondson (2012) writes, " . . . interpersonal fear frequently gives rise to poor decisions and incomplete execution" (p. 118). She continues:

> In psychologically safe environments, people believe that if they make a mistake, others will not penalize them or think less of them for it. They also believe that others will not resent or humiliate them when they ask for help or information. This belief comes about when people both trust and respect each other, and it produces a sense of confidence that the group won't embarrass, reject, or punish someone for speaking up. (pp. 118–119)

> *The relationship is really important in instructional coaching because without that relationship and without that trust, the teacher might want me to just tell her everything. Allowing the teacher to make those choices and the coach to respond to those choices depends on trust. I don't think we would have gotten to where we got to if the teachers and I didn't have that relationship.*
>
> —**Susan Leyden**, Instructional Coach, Beaverton, Oregon

As Bryk and Schneider (2002) have written, trust is "forged in daily social exchanges—trust grows over time through exchanges where the expectations held for others are validated in action" (pp. 136–137). Relational trust, Michael Fullan (2001) writes, includes "competence" as well as "respect, "personal regard for others," and "integrity" (p. 65).

Given this fact, when teachers are opposed to recording their lessons, the reason likely isn't the idea of being video-recorded but lack of trust. The remaining guidelines will help leaders increase the level of trust in their schools.

2. MAKE PARTICIPATION A CHOICE

Some leaders may be tempted to simply instruct their staff to record their classes and watch their lessons. However, forcing teachers to record their lessons and watch the video will almost certainly engender resentment and a negative attitude about the video. Telling people they must do something that they find unpleasant often leads to anxiety, resentment, anger, and resistance and significantly interferes with learning. Further, as explained elsewhere, if leaders genuinely want teachers to be professionals, they must give teachers meaningful choices, not take choices away (Knight, 2011).

Ensuring that teachers have meaningful choices does not mean that choosing not to learn is an option. Learning in any profession is, by definition, compulsory—professionals need to continuously improve; if not, they are acting unprofessionally.

Teachers especially need to have choices about how they learn. Getting a clear picture of reality is an essential part of professional learning, but that picture can be acquired in many ways (for example, review of student work, formative assessment data, or observation data). VPD should be just one of a menu of options open to them.

One particularly worrisome approach to compulsory video recording is to use video as a cheap substitute for walkthroughs and other forms of teacher evaluation. Administrators need to observe and evaluate the teachers in their classrooms. Further, as I explain in Chapter 6, when teachers agree, video can be a powerful part of the evaluation process. But cameras must serve as a tool for learning, not spying. When cameras are forced on people or used when people do not know they are on, they damage culture and trust, not enhance learning. The idea that a principal might have a monitor in his office and push a button to see what is happening in any classroom at any time is an Orwellian vision that should disturb anyone who loves children and learning.

3. FOCUS ON INTRINSIC MOTIVATION AND SAFETY

In worst-case scenarios, video might be used to apply pressure, extrinsically motivate, or, at worst, embarrass teachers as a way of pushing them toward improving their practice based on the rationale that people change only when they feel the pressure to change. However, such a primitive approach will likely make things worse, not better.

As researcher Theresa Amabile concluded after reviewing thousands of data points from surveys, interviews, and observations of many teams in corporations:

Managers who say—or secretly believe—that employees work better under pressure, uncertainty, unhappiness, or fear are just plain wrong. Negative inner work has a negative effect on the four dimensions of performance: people are less creative, less productive, less deeply committed to their work, and less collegial to each other when their inner work lives darken. (Amabile & Kramer, 2011, p. 58)

For video to be an effective tool, therefore, it must support and enhance teachers' intrinsic motivation to change. Done well, VPD unleashes a teacher's personal desire to achieve his or her personal best.

4. ESTABLISH BOUNDARIES

When we introduce VPD into a district, we must recognize that recording and watching oneself on video is complicated and personal. As Parker Palmer (2009) has written, "The things I teach are things I care about, and what I care about helps define my selfhood" (p. 17). When a conversation addresses topics related to who we are as persons, things get messy. For this reason, when setting up VPD, it is critical to be clear about boundaries, especially boundaries related to who sees a video and how people talk about it.

In our interviews with coaches, a major theme centered around the fact that teachers wanted to know who would watch the video before they agreed to be recorded. Teachers, coaches told us, were willing to be vulnerable and learn from recordings of their class, but they wanted assurance that their most vulnerable moments would not end up being posted on the school's homepage for all the world to see. In most settings, video recordings should be considered the property of the person being recorded and shared only when the teacher is completely at ease about them.

Possible Boundaries for Conversations

- Focus on data.
- Be nonjudgmental.
- Respect the complex nature of teaching.
- Be positive.
- Be respectful.
- Be supportive.
- Offer suggestions for improvement only after being asked.

Boundaries must also be established for conversations about video recordings, whether those conversations take place between teachers, a teacher and a coach, a teacher and an administrator, or teams of educators. For example, those discussing video recordings might agree that their comments must always focus on data, be nonjudgmental, and embody a respect for the complex nature of teaching. Additionally, stakeholders may agree to keep all conversations positive, respectful, and supportive and to offer suggestions for improvement only after being asked for feedback.

5. WALK THE TALK

If instructional coaches and administrators want others to take the brave step of watching themselves on video, they need to walk the talk by watching themselves on video, too. For example, coaches can record themselves coaching and then review the video to learn how they ask questions, listen, build relationships, find common ground, work from a partnership perspective, or carry out other aspects of coaching. Teams of coaches in a district could use video to collaboratively improve their teaching by sharing video and discussing what they see. More information about how coaches can use video to improve their teaching may be found in Chapter 3, and more on teams and video in Chapter 5.

Administrators and coaches who lead workshops or meetings could similarly record themselves in action and share their findings at follow-up sessions. What matters is that leaders authentically use video to get better at what they do in order to set an example for everyone.

In his presentations, coaching expert Steve Barkley suggests an innovative way for principals to encourage others to watch video recordings of themselves teaching. In schools that have coaches, Barkley suggests that principals teach a model lesson, video-record themselves teaching, and then show a section of the video during a staff meeting followed by a public session with an instructional coach, also during the meeting.

When a principal records herself and then participates in coaching, the message is clear: "I'm not asking you to do anything that I wouldn't do myself." Barkley mentions an added benefit. When a principal tells her staff that she is going to show them a lesson and subsequently be coached, everyone in the room will want to see what happens on the video and during coaching. "You might have a staff that loves to leave meetings as early as possible," Barkley notes, "but they'll stay to watch that."

6. GO SLOW TO GO FAST

It may be a cliché, but in this case, the saying is very applicable. If leaders move too quickly to push VPD, there is a great likelihood that their initiative will not succeed. Leaders need to take the time necessary to ensure that implementation of VPD follows the guidelines outlined previously.

One effective way to introduce VPD is to start with a few volunteer teachers who are interested in and willing to try out the camera. Often it is a good idea to begin with teachers who are considered informal leaders, those teachers whom others generally listen to in the school. In addition, certain simple messages need to be communicated again and again: VPD is a choice, not a requirement. Teachers own their video, and they have to share it only if they choose to do so. Perhaps the most important message is that learning is expected for all, but every professional has a great deal of choice around how he or she chooses to learn.

Setting Up Video-Enhanced Professional Development: Practical Concerns

In addition to the guidelines discussed above, some practical concerns must be considered before setting up VPD. Some of the more important ones are addressed in the following.

Type of Camera. As this book is being written, late 2013, there are many cameras available that are suitable for teachers, coaches, and administrators who plan to use video recording as a part of their professional learning. Flip cameras, iPads, digital cameras, GoPros, iPhones, Androids, and other smartphones may all be used to record lessons.

Most cameras yield valuable information. In general, I suggest using a camera you already own and are familiar with. If you are buying a new camera, however, the following questions are useful as a basis for making a sound purchasing decision:

- **What kind of lens do I need?** If the camera will be used primarily to capture an entire classroom, a fish-eye lens is best. Some cameras come with such a lens; for others, this type of lens may be purchased to be added on.
- **How important is sound?** Usually it is important to hear teachers and students clearly, so the sound quality of a recording is critical. Sound quality varies a great deal from one camera to another, so some research into this variable is recommended. Many teachers own cameras, so a lot of information can be gathered easily just by asking colleagues for advice. Since technology advances quickly, doing a search on the web or posting a question on Twitter can also yield valuable information.

- **How easy is it to use the camera?** Most modern cameras are extremely easy to use. If the camera involves pushing more than one button, the alleged benefits may not be worth the complexity for our purposes here. People are much more inclined to use technology that is easy to use.
- **How easy is it to share video?** If you are an instructional coach or administrator and you are going to record a teacher's class, you will need a way to transfer video so the teacher can view it. Recording even a short video requires a lot of memory, more memory than can be sent in a standard e-mail. Many of the coaches we interviewed used file-sharing sites to share their videos with coaches, usually either Dropbox or Google Drive. In addition, several sites have been created just for the purpose of sharing video, including Be a Smarter Cookie, Edthena, Sibme, and the Teaching Channel. Courtney Horton, an instructional coach, found that the easiest way was just to share her iPad with her collaborating teacher.

Where to Point the Camera. Where the camera is faced, of course, depends on what the viewer wants to learn. If I'm interested in how much wait time I allow students to ask questions, I want the camera pointed at me. If I am interested in my students' level of engagement, I want the camera pointed at my students (see the following "District Video Policy" section regarding guidelines on privacy and consent).

> **Questions to Ask When Choosing a Camera**
>
> 1. What kind of lens do I need?
> 2. How important is sound?
> 3. How easy is it to use the camera?
> 4. How easy is it to share the video?

Most people we interviewed tried to do a little of both. For example, if instructional coaches were doing the recording, they often recorded the teacher when she was leading discussion and then recorded students when they were involved in conversations for activities. Instructional coach Crista Anderson found a way to record the teacher and students even when she was not in the class. She put her iPad in the back corner of the room, from which the camera could view the front of the room, the teacher's desk, and the whiteboard, so she could see as much of the class as possible.

The first time a class is viewed, capturing the teacher and students is the best plan. Once the teacher has watched a video of her class, she will be better able to decide if she wants to focus on her students or herself or try to record both.

Who Should Record the Class? Once again, the simple answer is, it depends. If a teacher is collaborating with an instructional coach or a principal, then the coach or principal can video-record the class. An extra adult in the room can record students, record the teacher, and move the camera to capture whatever seems most meaningful at a particular point. When possible, it is helpful if the coach is present to record the class, since being in the class gives the coach information he cannot get just from viewing video.

But teachers don't always have an adult in the room who can record their lessons. An alternative is to have a student record the class, so long as the teacher determines that this will not interfere with the student's learning. Glen McLachlan, an administrator at Knox Grammar School in Sydney, Australia, was able to celebrate a student's ability with film and get a great video of his lesson by having a student who was especially interested in film record his class.

A final idea is simply to set the camera up at a fixed spot and turn it on before students enter the room. Many educators, like Crista above, just set up the camera and hit record. The most recent version of the iPad makes this easy, as it can be propped up on the standard cover.

How Much of a Class Should You Record? The length of video recorded by the educators we interviewed varied greatly. The shortest video was just over 10 minutes. The longest was more than 70 minutes, an entire block schedule unit. Most educators find that for the first video they record, more is better than less. As a general guideline, recording an entire lesson is probably worthwhile. But once the first video has been watched and a goal has been set, a shorter video is often all that is needed; in fact, to save time, a shorter video may be better. For example, if a teacher is trying to reduce how long transitions take at the start of a lesson, all he may need to record are the first few minutes of the lesson.

Instructional coach Jennifer Adams told us that she found it "more beneficial to focus on a certain aspect of a lesson, filming for a shorter amount of time, but then really digging into it." Especially at the beginning of coaching, Jennifer noted that "when teachers are a bit nervous watching themselves on video, it is easier to just

> *I feel the videos do a really nice job of capturing what it is like to be a student in my classroom. And that is helpful. I don't think I do that a lot. I think a lot about the variety of activities and engaging lessons and so on. But the actual practicality of being seated in my class; what it looks like; what I sound like; where I am moving around and those little things outside of instructional choices, that was really interesting for me to see and to get closer to that.*
>
> *After you watch video for a while, it becomes less about what you look like and sound like and more about what it is like to be a kid in your class.*
>
> —**Sara Langton**, Middle School Science Teacher, Beaverton, Oregon

do snippets and talk about those parts—more frequent filming, but shorter segments."

How to Keep Video From Being a Distraction. In most cases, students are not that distracted by video, contrary to what many imagine. I have been in many classrooms recording video for Talking About Teaching on the Teaching Channel, which involves two large cameras, a boom microphone, and sound and camera people, besides me, and in each case the students pretty much carried on with their learning as if nothing was happening. Nevertheless, there are a few steps to take to minimize any distractions from the presence of a camera in the room.

Lea Molzcan, who was an instructional coach on our first study, suggests telling the students about the camera at the start of the lesson and letting them play around a bit, so they won't be tempted to play around during the lesson.

> One of my most vocal kids noticed the camera at the start of class, and then everyone wanted to know what the camera was for and why I was taping them. So I told them what the camera was for and that they should get all their waves and giggles out. They didn't even look at it after that. Class just proceeded as normal.

Others suggest setting the camera up before students come into class. Many cameras are so small that they can be set up on a shelf and turned on without students even noticing that they are being recorded. In most situations, a quick explanation is all that is needed to keep students on track.

District Video Policy. Whenever I discuss video-recording lessons, people have concerns about privacy and consent. To ensure privacy, districts should establish policy around the use of video.

As a general guideline, the more people who will see a video, the more important consent will be. If a teacher records her lesson, watches it on her own, and no one else sees the lesson, likely consent is not an issue so long as the video can never become public. Similarly, if a coach or administrator records a class and shares the video only with the teacher in question, consent probably is not necessary since everyone watching the video also watched the class. Nevertheless, both of these situations and many others should be clarified through district policy.

Things become more complicated when the video becomes more public. What if a video is shown to a team of teachers? As a parent, would you want to know that a video of your children was being shared across a school? What if a video was placed on the Internet as an example of excellent teaching or learning? Would you want to know in advance?

My suggestion is that district leaders consider these questions carefully. First, a policy must be written to ensure that teachers are never forced to be recorded when they don't wish to be recorded. As mentioned elsewhere in this book, forcing teachers to record themselves when they are strongly opposed to it most likely will not lead to meaningful learning; and, equally important, forcing teachers to record themselves shows a lack of respect for their professionalism.

Second, policies and procedures must be established to ensure that parents' wishes are respected. Many schools send out a blanket consent form at the start of the year covering all ways in which students might be video-recorded. If parents don't want their children to be recorded, their wishes must be respected and their children seated off camera during classroom recordings. Many teachers will want to also consider the wishes of students themselves.

By thinking about when and how video will be recorded and shared, establishing policy, and communicating clearly with parents, leaders can ensure that educators are free to use video as a central part of their learning.

Turning Ideas Into Action

STUDENTS

Students can be and should be a big part of any effort to get better at teaching. Students can participate in a discussion about a given video. This may involve showing a clip to an entire class and asking for their thoughts on what they see. For example, a teacher who is studying questioning skills might show a brief recording of a few questions and ask students for their insights on how the questions affect them. Additionally, teachers might invite select students to stay after class for more in-depth discussion of teaching.

TEACHERS

The most important thing teachers can do is dive in and get started with video. This might take a period of desensitization, however. One way to get comfortable with video is to video-record oneself in private, less formal situations. For example, a teacher might record himself reading a story to his daughter or having a conversation with his wife or children. It may sound a bit silly, but the important thing is to get over the awkwardness of watching yourself on video. Once you are at ease with video—and that will almost inevitably happen—the real learning can begin.

COACHES

There are at least three actions coaches can take to increase the likelihood that they will get started in the most effective way. First, coaches need to learn about their technology. A lot of time will be lost if coaches incorrectly record and lose a lesson. Second, coaches need to get comfortable watching themselves on video, which can be done by recording simple conversations with friends and family at home. Finally, coaches need to clearly understand district policy about the use of video.

PRINCIPALS

To promote VPD, principals need constantly to communicate four messages: (a) VPD is a powerful way to accelerate learning, (b) how teachers use VPD is up to them, (c) VPD is not compulsory, and (d) learning is compulsory. To get the schools our students deserve, everyone in the school must be a learner.

SYSTEM LEADERS AND POLICY MAKERS

District leaders need to communicate across the school district and to the community that VPD is not a "big brother" form of strong-arm accountability but a form of professional development founded on a recognition of the professionalism of teachers. Additionally, system leaders need to establish clear policies that address most situations in which video recording might be implemented as a part of professional learning, including teachers recording themselves, coaches or administrators recording teachers and sharing video with them, teams of teachers watching video, and video being shared on the Internet for the general public to see.

TO SUM UP

Video will be introduced much more successfully when leaders:

- Establish trust before implementing video
- Make participation in video a choice

- Focus on intrinsic motivation and avoid pressure and embarrassment
- Establish boundaries for conversations to create a positive learning environment
- Walk the talk by using video for their own professional learning
- Increase success by starting out carefully, going slow to go fast

To set up a successful video-enhanced professional learning, leaders should consider

- The best type of camera to meet their educators' learning needs
- Where the camera should be pointed when lessons are recorded
- Who should record the class
- Recording at least 20 minutes of the class
- Setting up video so that it doesn't distract students
- Establishing district policy for the sharing of video

GOING DEEPER

Amy Edmondson's (2012) *Teaming: How Organizations Learn, Innovate, and Compete in the Knowledge Economy* is a great book about teams in general, but she especially makes the case, based on her research, that psychological safety is a vital component for any learning team. I think anyone leading groups of people will find the book helpful, and in *High-Impact Instruction* (Knight, 2013), I discuss how her ideas might be applied to leading groups of students.

Anthony Bryk and Barbara Schneider's (2005) *Trust in Schools: A Core Resource for Improvement* is recognized as a classic text on the importance of trust in schools. Based on their study of 12 Chicago schools over a 3-year period, the authors conclude that trust both between staff and parents and between administrators and staff is essential for improvement in schools.

Teresa Amabile and Steve Kramer's (2011) *The Progress Principle: Using Small Wins to Ignite Joy, Engagement, and Creativity at Work* is another excellent research-based description of the characteristics of effective teams. The book describes how to set up a learning environment in which continuous progress fuels a self-reinforcing cycle of growth, both within each individual and within an organization. This thought-provoking book also contains many practical suggestions for any leader.

Henry Cloud and John Townsend's (2004) *Boundaries: When to Say Yes, When to Say No—To Take Control of Your Life* is a classic work on boundaries in personal life and relationships. While the book is written from an explicit Christian point of view that some will find inconsistent with their worldview, its major merit lies in its presentation of a commonsense perspective that is consistent with most perspectives on life. If you are interested in establishing boundaries, this is an important book to read.

The researchers at the Harvard Negotiation Project have written many useful books about negotiation and interpersonal communication, including a clear articulation of the importance of autonomy within interactions. Roger Fisher and Daniel Shapiro's (2006) *Beyond Reason: Using Emotions as You Negotiate* and Roger Fisher and Scott Brown's (1989) *Getting Together: Building Relationships as We Negotiate* both make the case for respecting autonomy while also offering excellent suggestions for improving any kind of interactions.

Several websites have been established to make it easier for educators to share video. Some sites to consider include the following:

http://sibme.com

https://www.beasmartercookie.com

http://www.edthena.com

https://www.teachingchannel.org

Chapter 3: Instructional Coaches

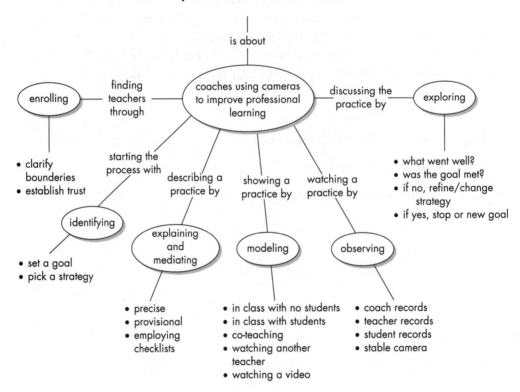

3

INSTRUCTIONAL COACHES

Coaching done well may be the most effective intervention designed for human performance.

—Atul Gawande

Using video during coaching is like the gas in the car. Video helps you move forward, and it's easier and quicker. If you don't have gas in the car, you can't move forward at all. Video is like stepping on the accelerator.

—Amanda Trimble, Instructional Coach,
Noblesville, Indiana

When Melissa Hickey was offered the chance to be an instructional coach, she didn't think she wanted the job. "I really didn't want to be an instructional coach. I didn't want to be out of the classroom," she said. Melissa "absolutely loved" working with the children in her school, but the miles she had to drive to work were too long, and when an instructional coaching position "kind of presented itself . . . closer to home," she decided to take the job at a new school, the Greater Hartford Academy of the Arts Elementary Magnet School in Hartford, Connecticut.

Melissa "was a little scared about starting a new job." At first, she said, "I had no idea what I was doing. For the first month and a half at the new school, I opened a lot of boxes and delivered a lot of supplies until we all got our feet on the ground. I thought I was a pretty good teacher, but I was worried that I wouldn't be able to do my job."

Melissa went to a workshop on video and coaching during her second month on the job. She thought video was interesting and decided to try it at her school. At first she met "resistance from a couple of teachers. Nobody wants to be videotaped. Nobody wants to see it," she commented. But Melissa made sure teachers knew, as she expressed it, "that they were going to have all the power." Teachers had the option to keep or delete the video. "It wouldn't go further than me or them. There were times when a teacher didn't want me to video-record them, so I would offer to video-record the students."

Melissa was very surprised at "how quickly the teachers all came around to agreeing to be video-recorded." At first she worked one on one with teachers. "I would have them view the video by themselves, and then we would meet the next day and talk about it." Video helped teachers see many things that they would not otherwise have noticed. "One teacher," Melissa said,

> spoke very, very fast, but until she saw the video of herself, she never realized how fast she spoke. Once she saw it, though, she was able to correct it immediately. I think it only takes seeing yourself on video once or twice to get over the initial shyness or reluctance. After that you can kind of let it go and really focus on the teaching. They all loved the fact that they could see themselves. I think video breaks down a lot of walls.

For Melissa, it was important to ensure that the teachers knew they could trust her. "Initially, I think they were all a little apprehensive, and they thought it might become a punitive thing," she said.

> The big thing I learned as a coach is that you have to let the teachers decide what they want to work on, what happens to the videos, what videos to take, etc. Give them options so they don't feel this is being imposed on them. Make it clear that this is confidential, not evaluative, but for best teaching. It can't be that today is a videotaping day and I have to put on my high heels and best dress.

After a few weeks, teachers started sharing snippets of video at grade-level team meetings. Eventually, everyone was willing to let

Melissa show the videos, and using them deepened the quality and meaning of the collaborative conversations and built a true community among the staff. "I think it has brought them all closer," Melissa concluded, "because they were able to see their good and their not-so-good teaching. Everyone saw everyone else being courageous in showing video. They were willing to be vulnerable with each other, which brought the grade-level teams together."

> The collaboration opened up a lot of lines of communication. We were all just kind of in it together for these deep conversations. Best of all, the teaching got much better. Video allowed us to see ourselves as we truly were. It allowed us to collaborate. It allowed us to focus on certain aspects of our teaching and go a lot deeper with that. We all saw each other improve. Seeing a brand-new teacher get better at classroom management throughout the year and getting better at teaching—that was big. We had many new teachers in the school. Video was a really effective way to meet the needs of a lot of teachers at a lot of different levels.

Now, after a year coaching, Melissa reports that she is much more comfortable being a coach. "What I didn't expect was that I would learn as much as I did coaching. Sometimes I think I learned a lot more than the teachers I'm supposed to be coaching. I'm really excited to be a coach now. I'm excited to keep going with what we have started. I'm excited to get better at it. We can move forward and get even better."

Instructional coaches like Melissa Hickey have been the focus of study for my colleagues and me at the Kansas Coaching Project for the past 15 years. Our interest in coaching has grown out of a basic understanding and recognition: *Without follow-up, professional learning likely won't change instruction.*

Over more than a decade, we've conducted studies to refine and validate instructional coaching. Using a variation on design research, which we refer to as lean design research, we are continuously trying to simplify and improve our model for coaching. The most significant finding we have uncovered so far is that video recording makes instructional coaching easier and more effective. Video recording was not a part of coaching when we started studying it, but in the course of our work we have learned that it can have a huge, positive impact on the whole process.

Video 3.1
An Overview of Coaching Using Video

www.corwin.com/ focusonteaching

Video-Enhanced Instructional Coaching

Using video as part of coaching involves much more than simply turning the camera on and later talking about what the video shows. If they want to make an impact, coaches using cameras must understand how complex it is for teachers to watch themselves do what they do. A few years back a teacher in Alberta, Canada, helped me understand why it is often difficult at first for teachers to watch themselves teach. He told me that when he was on the wrestling team in college, he and his coach used to go over video of him wrestling almost every week. "Watching that video of myself wrestling wasn't a big deal," he said. "In fact, I looked forward to it. But watching video of myself teaching, that is an entirely different thing."

What is the difference between watching yourself playing a sport and watching yourself teaching? The answer is likely the complexity of the work.[1] When we get feedback on technical skills, such as how to position ourselves while playing a sport, we are less inclined to take the feedback personally. However, when we get feedback on more complex or artful practices, we are more inclined to be defensive about what we hear. For example, suggestions on classroom management are usually harder to listen to than suggestions on how to use a computer program. When the topic turns to complex skills, the conversation becomes more difficult. Talking about messy problems usually is messy.

More than a decade ago, Heifetz and Linksy (2002) enhanced our understanding of the complexity of tasks. They explained the importance of distinguishing between simple and complex challenges, which they referred to as "technical" and "adaptive" problems, respectively.

> Every day, people have problems for which they do, in fact, have the necessary know-how and procedures. We call these technical problems. But there is a whole host of problems that are not amenable to authoritative expertise or standard operating procedures. They cannot be solved by someone who provides answers from on high. We call these adaptive challenges because they require experiments, new discoveries, and adjustments from numerous places in the organization or community. (p. 13)

---

[1] For an insightful discussion of the complexity of a task and the quality of performance, see Chapter 3 in Atul Gawande's *The Checklist Manifesto: How to Get Things Right* (2011).

According to Heifetz and Linksy (2002), "the single most common source of leadership failure . . . is that people, especially those in positions of authority, treat adaptive challenges like technical problems" (p. 14).

When we ignore the difference between simple and complex problems by, for example, suggesting that teachers simply listen to instructional coaches the way athletes listen to athletic coaches, we risk creating a coaching model that is twice doomed for failure: first, because addressing complex challenges as if they were simple skills increases the likelihood of resistance, and second because technical solutions for adaptive problems likely won't work.

Video recording addresses both of these issues. First, when we video-record a class, the video captures the rich complexity of the classroom. As middle school English teacher Lea Molzcan told us, "looking at a recording of your class is like looking into a kaleidoscope because there are so many things happening. What you see keeps changing and evolving." Additionally, instructional coaching that employs video responds to the complexities of teaching by adapting to that complexity over time. Coach and teacher set a goal based on the picture of reality revealed in video of the class. They monitor progress toward the goal by recording and watching video of teaching and learning, adapt their strategies for hitting the goal based on what the video reveals, and then continue learning together until they hit the goal.

Instructional coaching is not a one-size-fits-all approach; instructional coaches adapt solutions to the unique opportunities and challenges each teacher experiences.

Video Increases Trust

Perhaps the most frequent comment we heard in the interviews conducted for this book is that teachers need to trust their coaches in order to agree to being recorded. As instructional coach Melissa Hickey explained, "There has to be a certain amount of trust between the coach and the teachers. Teachers have to be able to say, 'No, I don't want to be videotaped' or, 'No, today is just not a good day.' They have to be comfortable with video." Of course, if teachers don't trust their coaches, coaching of any sort will most likely be unproductive anyway.

However, one of the surprise findings from our interviews is that coaches and teachers both reported that video actually strengthens colleagues' relationships and increases trust. Instructional coach

Courtney Horton said she felt that using video during coaching "helped strengthen my partnership with teachers because it is something we are going through together. It's a growth process for us both to watch video and talk about it together. Video is a great nonevaluative, reflective tool that has deepened my partnerships with my teachers."

Courtney's comments suggest two reasons video might increase trust. First, when coaches and teachers base their conversations on video, they work from a shared understanding of current reality in the classroom. If teachers haven't seen a video of the classroom, they may understand the classroom differently than the coach does. As I have pointed out throughout this book, we usually have a poor understanding of what it looks like when we do what we do. As a result, if teachers haven't seen video recordings of their lessons, they may not see the relevance of their coaches' comments and dismiss what a coach says. When coach and teacher both see the lesson the same way, however, they can engage in real, meaningful dialogue about learning.

"Video," Kristen Shrout Fernandes, an instructional coach from Central Falls, Rhode Island, said, "is a really important tool for building shared understanding. It helps ensure that both the coaches and the teachers are on the same page. Sometimes you may be talking about something and the other person may not fully understand what you are trying to say. Watching video changes this. Now people say, 'Oh, so that is what you're talking about.'"

A second reason video increases trust is that when coach and teacher set a goal based on video, collaborate to implement a teaching practice, monitor progress by viewing video recordings of a class, and eventually hit the goal based on clear evidence from video, both have a shared sense of accomplishment based on real-life evidence. Coaching based on video is coaching that is real, and coach and teacher feel a real sense of accomplishment when their collaboration leads to better learning for students.

Video Facilitates Partnership Coaching

Video also enables an important change in the way coach and teacher interact. For some, coaching involves top-down interactions with an expert giving feedback and advice to an apprentice. During such a top-down approach, the coach observes the teacher, identifies what is going well and what the teacher needs to do to improve, and then makes suggestions. Essentially, during top-down coaching, the coach does most of the thinking, decides what the teacher needs to do, and then tries to get the teacher to agree to do it.

There are a number of problems with this top-down model. First, as Kegan and Lahey (2001) have explained, top-down interactions are grounded in two problematic assumptions:

> The first [assumption] is that the perspective of the feedback giver (let's call him the supervisor)—what he sees and thinks, his feedback—is right, is correct. An accompanying assumption is that there is only one correct answer. When you put these two assumptions together, they amount to this: the supervisor has the one and only correct view of the situation. (We call this "the super vision assumption"; that is, the supervisor has *super vision*). (p. 128)

When coaches work from "super vision assumptions," they limit how much they learn from the person who knows most about the classroom: the teacher. The classroom teacher is in class every day and usually knows an enormous amount about each student. Coach and teacher arrive at better solutions when the teacher's knowledge, insights, and ideas are a part of the coaching conversation—that is, coaching leads to better solutions when teachers have a voice in coaching.

An equally significant problem with top-down feedback is that it often engenders resistance. As I have written elsewhere in this book and in *Unmistakable Impact* in particular (Knight, 2011), when teachers are told, explicitly or implicitly, that their opinion doesn't matter, that coaching is compulsory, and that they must implement practices that have been chosen for them, they resist. A more effective model is one that positions teachers as equal partners in the coaching process (see Figure 3.1; Knight, 2007, 2011).[2]

Instructional coaching based on partnership is an alternative to top-down coaching (see Figure 3.2). During this approach, which is much easier to implement using video recordings, the coach is not positioned as an expert with "super vision" but as a partner who engages in dialogue with teachers about what they see on video and what they want to do to move forward. Video recordings, much like Thinking Prompts in the classroom, described in *High-Impact*

---

[2]Sadly, a recent survey conducted by the Gallup organization of more than 100,000 employees in a wide variety of occupations found that teachers are the "least likely" to say, "at work my opinion seems to count" (http://www.gallup.com).

Figure 3.1 Top-Down Coaching

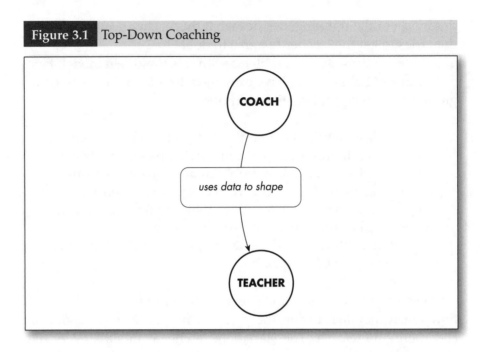

Instruction (Knight, 2013), become what Parker Palmer (2009) refers to as "third things":

> "[T]hird things" . . . represent neither the voice of the facilitator nor the voice of the participant . . . Rightly used, a third thing functions a bit like the old Rorschach inkblot test, evoking from us whatever the soul wants us to attend to. (pp. 92–93)

Video functions as a third thing throughout the coaching process, representing, to paraphrase Palmer, neither the voice of the instructional coach nor the voice of the teacher. Teacher and coach equally interpret video, identify a goal (sometimes looking at video of others teaching the practice to be implemented), monitor progress by watching video, and use video as a point of departure for all coaching conversations. As Amanda Trimble, an instructional coach from Noblesville, Indiana, told us, "Using video made it so that the conversation wasn't about me and what I thought; it had more to do with the teacher and what she felt was good for her students."

> *Using video recording is a way to see things clearer, but it is also a tool that brought me closer to some of the teachers. It was something we could use together. It wasn't their view or my view; it was something we could share. It was a way to connect.*
>
> —**Tara Strahan**, Instructional Coach, Orange City, Florida

Figure 3.2   Partnership Coaching

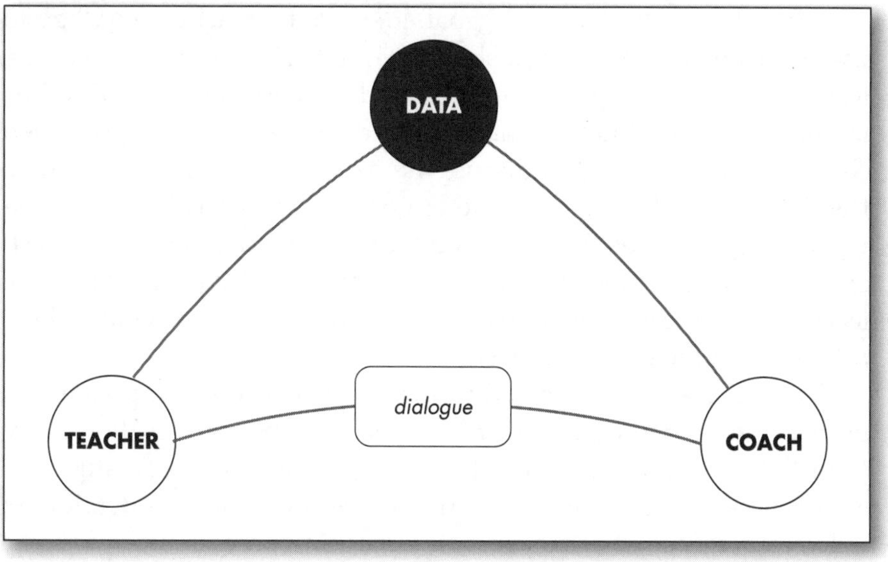

Video and the Components of Instructional Coaching

For more than a decade, I have worked with researchers, coaches, and educators to refine the process instructional coaches use when they collaborate with teachers. Although each coaching session is different depending on the teacher, a coach can increase the chance that there will be lasting impact by undertaking certain activities.

The instructional coaching process is pretty straightforward. Once a teacher is enrolled in coaching, the coach and teacher collaborate to identify a goal (a measurable change the teacher would like to see in student achievement, behavior, or attitude). Then coach and teacher identify a teaching strategy the teacher will implement to try to hit the goal, usually a strategy drawn from a collection of effective teaching practices such as those described in *High-Impact Instruction* (Knight, 2013). Following this, the coach precisely describes the practice, often using a checklist, and works with the teacher to modify the practice to tailor it to the teacher's unique strengths and her students' unique needs. The teacher then observes a model of the

Components of Instructional Coaching

1. Enroll
2. Identify
3. Explain and mediate
4. Model
5. Observe
6. Explore

practice, perhaps by watching the coach teaching in the classroom, watching a video, or observing another teacher using the practice.

After the teacher has set a goal, identified a teaching strategy to try, and learned the strategy, she tries it out. The coach observes the teacher implementing the practice and gathers data on what the teacher does and whether that will lead to reaching the goal. Then coach and teacher meet to discuss the data. If the goal has been met, teacher and coach can start another goal or take a break from coaching. If the goal has not been met, on the other hand, teacher and coach explore how to refine the practice so that it will better enable the teacher to hit the goal or choose another practice, repeating the whole process until the goal is reached.

Video increases the effectiveness of each of the components of instructional coaching and turns the focus of the conversation away from the coach's opinion and toward what matters most: students' experiences in the classroom. In the rest of this chapter, I detail how video can be used at each step of the coaching process.[3]

1. ENROLL

During the "enroll" component of coaching, coaches use several strategies to enlist teachers for coaching. For example, they have one-to-one conversations, give presentations to small groups of teachers or the entire school, hold informal conversations, write articles/announcements in school/district newsletters, or follow up on principal referrals. (More about this component of coaching, and all others, is found in *Instructional Coaching* [Knight, 2007].)

Generally, people embrace coaching when they are convinced that it will lead to changes that are rewarding and that they think they can easily implement (Knight, 2011; Patterson et al., 2013). When coaches are enrolling teachers for coaching that involves video, there are some additional issues to talk about. First, coaches should explain that the main purpose of the video is to ensure that coaching focuses on what is most helpful to the teacher and the students. "If we get a clear picture of what's happening in the class through the use of video," the coach can explain, "we'll have a better chance of doing what will have the biggest impact."

Coaches should also emphasize that the video will not be shared with anyone other than those whom the teacher chooses. Instructional coach Melissa Hickey told us that "there has to be trust between the

---

[3]For more information on the components of instructional coaching, see *Instructional Coaching* (Knight, 2007).

coach and the teacher, and that means the teacher has to be able to say "I want the video" or "I don't want the video shown to anyone." Teachers also have to be able to say "Today is just not a good day."

To build trust, coaches need to reinforce that the video is only being recorded to help the teacher accomplish her goals; the teacher chooses where to point the camera, who views the video (usually only the coach and teacher), and what happens to the video after its immediate use. Collaborating teachers are much more at ease when they know that video is only for their use.

2. IDENTIFY

During this component of coaching, the teacher collaborates with the coach to set a goal and select a strategy to try to meet that goal. This is the most important component of instructional coaching, because if teacher and coach do not pick a goal that can make a difference for students, a lot of time will be wasted. To be worth the effort, coaching must lead to real improvements in students' lives, and without an appropriate goal, significant changes may not come about.

> **The Components of Coaching**
>
> - Enroll teachers in coaching.
>
> - Explain the purpose of the video.
>
> - Clarify that the teacher chooses who will see the recording— usually only the teacher and coach.
>
> - Let the teacher choose where to place the camera, what to do with the video, and which camera to use.

To ensure that teachers identify a useful goal and appropriate strategies, coaches follow a series of simple steps during this component of coaching. First, the coach helps the teacher get a clear picture of reality, often by video-recording the teacher's class. Then, together, coach and teacher identify a change the teacher would like to see in student behavior, achievement, or attitude and set a measurable goal. Following this, they identify a teaching strategy the teacher will try out to hit the strategy.

Get a Clear Picture of Reality. A shared, accurate view of reality is necessary to identify a meaningful goal. This is more difficult than it might seem because, as Bossidy and Charan (2004) have written, "avoiding reality is a basic and ubiquitous human tendency" (p. 26). When coaches use cameras, they video-record a teacher's class to capture what is happening during a lesson. "The video," as coach Amanda Trimble told us, "helps the teacher reflect because it is real, authentic evidence. You can't disagree with a video of what happened in your class."

Usually the coach asks the teacher to choose the class he wants recorded, encouraging the teacher to suggest the class that will yield the most useful information. Most coaches we interviewed video-recorded both the teacher and students, moving the camera back and forth—focusing on the teacher when he led discussion and on the students when they were doing most of the talking.

After the video is recorded, the coach and teacher watch the video. In our research, we have found that it is best that they watch the video separately because that way (a) the teacher watches the video without concern for what someone else thinks of the video; (b) the teacher can watch the video at his own pace, stopping and starting whenever he wishes; and (c) coach and teacher can engage in more meaningful conversations when they have both watched the video ahead of time and don't have to divide their attention between the video and their colleague.

We have created three documents that coaches can share with teachers to help them get the most out of their video. The first document, Figure 3.3, gives teachers some pointers on what to look for when they watch their video. To help teachers get a clearer picture of how their students are learning, coaches can share Figure 3.4, the Watch Your Students form. Finally, to help teachers get a clearer picture of how they are teaching, coaches can share Figure 3.5, the Watch Yourself form.

Identify a Change the Teacher Wants to See and Set a Measurable Goal. After the coach and teacher have watched the video separately, they meet to talk about what they noticed in the video. The goal of this conversation is to identify a goal (outcome) that the teacher would like to see in the students. We recommend selecting as a goal a measurable change in student achievement, behavior, or attitude. To guide the teacher to identifying such a goal, the coach might pose the following questions:

1. On a scale of 1 to 10, how close was the lesson to your ideal?

2. What would have to change to make the class closer to a 10?

3. What would your students be doing?

4. What would that look like?

5. How would we measure that?

6. Do you want that to be your goal?

7. Would it really matter to you if you hit that goal?

8. What teaching strategy will you try to hit that goal?

Figure 3.3   How to Get the Most Out of Watching Your Video

Goal

Identify two sections of the video that you like and one or two sections of video you'd like to further explore.

Getting Ready

Watching themselves on video is one of the most powerful strategies professionals can use to improve their performance. However, it can be a challenge. It takes a little time to get used to seeing yourself on screen, so be prepared for a bit of a shock. After a while, you will become more comfortable with the process.

- Find a place to watch where you won't be distracted.

- You may find it helpful to read through the Watch Your Students (Figure 3.4) and Watch Yourself (Figure 3.5) forms to remind yourself of things to keep in mind while watching.

- Set aside a block of time so you can watch the video uninterrupted.

- Make sure you've got a pen and paper ready to take notes.

Watching the Video

- Plan to watch the entire video in one sitting.

- Take notes on anything that you find interesting.

- Remember to write the time from the video beside any note you make so that you can return to it if you wish.

- People tend to be hard on themselves, so be sure to watch for things you like in the video.

- After watching the video, review your notes and circle the items you will discuss with your coach (two you like and one or two you would like to further explore).

- Sit back, relax, and enjoy the experience.

Figure 3.4   Watch Your Students Form

Watch Your Students

Date:

After watching the video of today's class, please rate how close the behavior of your students is to your goal for an ideal class in the following areas:

	Not Close						*Right On*
Students were engaged in learning (90% engagement is recommended).	1	2	3	4	5	6	7
Students interacted respectfully.	1	2	3	4	5	6	7
Students clearly understand how they are supposed to behave.	1	2	3	4	5	6	7
Students rarely interrupted each other.	1	2	3	4	5	6	7
Students engaged in high-level conversation.	1	2	3	4	5	6	7
Students clearly understand how well they are progressing (or not).	1	2	3	4	5	6	7
Students are interested in learning activities in the class.	1	2	3	4	5	6	7

Comments:

This form is available for download at **www.corwin.com/focusonteaching.**

Figure 3.5 Watch Yourself Form

Watch Yourself

Date:

After watching the video of today's class, please rate how close your instruction is to your ideal in the following areas:

	Not Close					Right On	
My praise-to-correction ratio was at least a 3 to 1.	1	2	3	4	5	6	7
I clearly explained expectations prior to each activity.	1	2	3	4	5	6	7
My corrections were calm, consistent, immediate, and planned in advance.	1	2	3	4	5	6	7
My questions were at the appropriate level (know, understand, do).	1	2	3	4	5	6	7
My learning structures (stories, cooperative learning, thinking devices, experiential learning) were effective.	1	2	3	4	5	6	7
I used a variety of learning structures effectively.	1	2	3	4	5	6	7
I clearly understand what my students know and don't know.	1	2	3	4	5	6	7

Comments:

Choose a Teaching Strategy to Use to Hit the Goal. Once a measurable goal has been established, coach and teacher need to select a teaching strategy that the teacher will implement to achieve the goal. The strategy may be drawn from books such as Marzano's (2007) *Art and Science of Teaching*, Saphier, Haley-Speca, and Gower's (2008) *The Skillful Teacher*, Lemov's (2010) *Teach Like a Champion*, or my *High-Impact Instruction* (Knight, 2013).

In *High-Impact Instruction*, 16 teaching strategies are organized around the Big Four Framework:

- Content Planning
  - Guiding Questions
  - Learning Maps
- Formative Assessment
  - Identifying Specific Proficiencies
  - Choose a Way to Assess the Proficiency
  - Modify Teaching
- Instruction
  - Thinking Prompts
  - Effective Questions
  - Cooperative Learning
  - Stories
  - Authentic Learning
- Community Building
  - Learner-Friendly Culture
  - Power With, Not Power Over
  - Freedom Within Form
  - Expectations
  - Witness to the Good
  - Fluent Corrections

> *Video helps us stay grounded and pay closer attention to what is going on. We think about what changes we can make rather than me just sharing my observations and suggestions for how to change things. Since we are both looking at the same thing, it's not just me talking about what I noticed, it's "let's share what we both noticed."*
>
> —**Kirsten Shrout Fernandes,** Instructional Coach, Central Falls, Rhode Island

3. EXPLAIN AND MEDIATE

The goal during this component of coaching is for the coach to explain the new teaching practice and then help the teacher plan how to implement it. Thus, if a coach was explaining learning maps (for more information, see Chapter 2 of *High-Impact Instruction* [Knight, 2013]), the coach likely would need to explain the characteristics of a quality learning map, how to introduce the map at the start of a unit, how to use it to open and close daily lessons, and how to use it during an end-of-unit review.

During the explaining part, instructional coaches must make sure their explanations are precise and clear. If they cannot explain something clearly, the teacher they are coaching won't be able to implement it. Teachers can implement only what they hear and understand.

One way to increase the clarity of an explanation is to use checklists. A checklist is not a dumbing down of the explanation; instead, it distills an explanation to its essence. Indeed, if a coach cannot describe a practice through the use of a checklist, chances are that he does not understand the practice clearly enough.

Using a checklist to explain a practice does not mean that a coach expects the teacher to do it exactly as explained. As Eric Liu (2004) wrote, "Teaching is not one-size-fits-all; it's one-size-fits-one" (p. 47). Expecting a practice to always work the same way in every class is unrealistic given the complexity of the classroom.

For that reason, we suggest that coaches be precise but provisional when explaining a practice. That is, they explain the elements of the checklist clearly but ask the teacher how she might want to modify it to best meet the needs of her students or to best take advantage of her strengths as a teacher.

If the teacher wants to modify a practice, that is her decision. She knows her students best, and she is the one who will be using the teaching strategy. Further, if the teacher hits the goal, then whether she modifies the practice is irrelevant. Indeed, using her experience and understanding of students, she may have improved the practice.

However, if the goal is not met, coach and teacher can revisit the checklist to see if the implementation of the practice needs to be refined to better meet the goal. That way, the coach does not end up being in the one-up position of telling the teacher what to do.

In the mediation part of this component, the coach helps the teacher get ready to teach the chosen practice. In other words, the coach serves as a mediator between the practice as it is written down in a manual, book, or checklist and the teacher's classroom.

For a learning map, this might involve the following. First, a coach might use a checklist as a guideline to help the teacher create a learning map for a unit she is about to teach. Then the coach might use a checklist to help the teacher get ready to introduce the map at the start of the unit. Subsequently, the coach could use additional checklists to prepare the teacher to introduce and close lessons and to lead an end-of-unit review.

Throughout this component of coaching, the coach can also use video that has previously been recorded to show the teacher what a given practice looks like. Some coaches, with the permission of their colleagues, gather a library of practices from recordings. Similarly, some districts are creating central libraries of video for all faculty to view. Online sites such as the Teaching Channel also provide video that can be used.

4. MODEL

In most cases, to learn a practice, teachers need to see it. In *Influencer*, Patterson (2013) and his colleagues summarize research that shows "how powerfully our behavior is shaped by observing others" (p. 18). My research on coaching has led me to the same conclusion. During one study in which I interviewed 13 first- and second-year teachers in a middle school, every teacher told me that modeling was an extremely helpful part of coaching. One teacher spoke for the group when she said, "When she [the coach] came into the classroom, that's what helped me most. I could see that my students could be managed, not controlled, but managed . . . It was just one hour, but since I've had that experience, I know what to look for."[4]

The coaches in our coaching cohort research study taught us that modeling can occur in at least five different ways.

In the Classroom. Most commonly, the coach demonstrates the chosen practice in the collaborating teacher's classroom. Teachers have told us that they prefer that coaches don't teach the whole lesson but only the practice itself. Instructional coaches who model practices may want to video themselves teaching and then share the recording with the teacher. If time permits, they may wish to watch the video with the collaborating teacher.

In the Classroom With No Students. Some teachers prefer that the coach model a practice in the classroom without students being present. In that case, the coach shares the practice in the way he would if he was teaching the lesson. For example, the coach might use the "I do it, we do it, you do it" approach and show the teacher exactly how to teach it. Again, video may be used to make a record of the lesson that the teacher could review or that coach and teacher could discuss, perhaps right after the model lesson.

[4]You can read a download of these interviews at http://www.instructionalcoach .org/images/downloads/research-pubs/TeacherInterviews.pdf.

Co-Teaching. In some cases, such as when the lesson involves a content area that is unfamiliar to the coach, coach and teacher may co-teach. Again, video can be used to record the lesson so coach and teacher can explore how the teacher taught the practice and whether it worked. More information on how to discuss video is included in the Explore section below.

Visiting Another Teacher's Class. In some cases, especially if the goal is to learn a procedure (such as how to set students up for learning circles) or a management technique (such as how to correct or reinforce students), teachers may choose to see a practice by visiting another teacher's classroom. This is best when the teacher being observed has had a prior conversation with the visiting teacher and they have discussed a checklist that summarizes the practices.

Under such circumstances, the instructional coach may not be able to observe the class, and even if the coach observes the class with the teacher, the coach and teacher will be able to have only limited conversations while the class is being taught. For that reason, if the teacher being observed consents, the coach or teacher might video-record the lesson so they can review it later and get a deeper understanding of how to teach the practice. Even if the coach is unable to visit the classroom with the teacher, they can still discuss the video after the class if the presenting teacher agrees.

Watching Video. A final way to see a model of how to teach a practice is to watch a video. Sometimes the video is available on a video-sharing site like teachingchannel.org. At other times, the video is one the coach took of himself or of another teacher (with explicit approval of the teacher). What matters is that the teacher gets to see an example, or several examples, of how to teach the practice. After that, it is time for the teacher to try out the practice herself.

5. OBSERVE

Video makes it much easier for coaches to gather data on how a teacher implements practice or strategy. Without video, a coach has to take copious notes or gather specific data such as those described in Chapter 4, including time on task, ratio of interaction (praise vs. correction), instructional and noninstructional time, and so forth. The biggest problem with this approach is that since many teachers don't know what it looks like when they teach, they may not see how data, notes, or comments relate to the way they teach. When the class is recorded, however, both teacher and coach have an accurate, shared understanding of what happened in the classroom.

There are many ways a coach can record a class. In most classrooms, as coach Courtney Horton told us, students quickly forget there is a camera in the room. Nevertheless, a coach must make every effort to avoid causing distractions by standing or sitting out of the students' sight lines. What the coach records is the teacher's decision; it's her data, but often the coach records the teacher while she is teaching and the students while they are interacting. Thus, the coach moves the camera back and forth between teacher and students.

We recommend that the coach record the class, since no matter how much information a camera gathers, the coach is bound to miss something if not present in the classroom. Watching a video of a class without having been there is like watching a sporting event on television vs. watching it live in the stadium. There is much more to see and feel when your view extends beyond the scope of a lens.

Additionally, sometimes the coach must be in a teacher's class to gather data that show whether the teacher has met her goal. For example, if a teacher has set the goal of achieving 90% time on task, the coach has to be in class to gather the data.

Despite the advantages of observing a class, sometimes it is impossible for a coach to record a class, perhaps because of a schedule conflict, lack of time, or because the teacher prefers otherwise. In such situations, the camera can either be held by a student or set up and turned on to record a class before the students arrive. In this way, even if not optimal, cameras make it easier for coaches to meet the needs of larger numbers of teachers and students.

6. EXPLORE

During the "explore" phase of coaching, the coach and teacher talk about what happened when the new practice was implemented to determine what the teacher's next action should be. As depicted in Figure 3.6, action is based on whether the teacher has hit the identified goal.

As explained in the section on identifying a goal, it is most effective when the coach and teacher watch the video separately. Both should watch the video with the surveys in mind and come to the conversation prepared to discuss their answers. If checklists exist for looking at the behavior, they should be completed by both coach and teacher. Additionally, the coach might look for sections of the video

Figure 3.6 Exploring What Happened

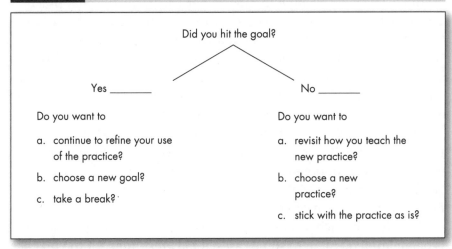

Did you hit the goal?

Yes _____   No _____

Do you want to

a. continue to refine your use
    of the practice?

b. choose a new goal?

c. take a break?

Do you want to

a. revisit how you teach the
    new practice?

b. choose a new
    practice?

c. stick with the practice as is?

that went very well as well as sections that she would like to explore separately. To make this process as simple and fast as possible, both coach and teacher need to keep track of the minute mark at which each of the sections occurs.

When teacher and coach meet, they should discuss each of the questions above. Many coaches like to begin by asking the teacher what he thought went well. Following this, the coach and teacher often discuss whether the goal was met. Sometimes this means that the coach shares data that she gathered in the classroom; at other times this means that coach and teacher look over student work or students' responses on formative assessments or compare notes on what they saw in the video. (If they are looking at a goal related to student responses, it is important that the sound quality of the video allows coach and teacher to hear all the student responses.)

If the teacher has reached the goal, the coach and teacher discuss whether he wants to set and pursue another goal or take a break from coaching. For example, a teacher who is about to take on coaching the basketball team may want to hold off on another goal. Similarly, near the end of the year, a teacher may want to wait until after the holidays to take on a new goal.

Explore Questions

- What are you pleased about?

- Did you hit the goal?

- If the goal was hit, do you want to identify another goal, take a break, or keep refining the current new practice?

- If the goal was not hit, do you want to stick with the chosen practice or try a new one?

- If you stick with the chosen practice, how will you modify it to increase its impact? (Revisit the checklist.)

- If you choose another practice, what will it be?

- What are your next actions?

If the teacher has not hit the goal, she has many options. For example, she can continue to modify her use of the original practice. This usually means revisiting the checklist with the coach to discuss how the practice might be adapted to better meet the needs of the students. If the teacher chooses to modify the teaching practice in significant ways, she and the coach can discuss teaching the practice with more fidelity. In some cases, the teacher may want to see a model or models of the practice being implemented.

Another option is to stop implementing the original practice and try another one. If this is the teacher's choice, usually the coach and teacher discuss options and then the coach repeats the "explain," "mediate," and "model" components of coaching to ensure the teacher is ready to implement the new practice.

Finally, the teacher may choose to continue with the practice as it is being implemented. In some cases, it may take time for the practice to have the desired impact. In other words, sometimes changing nothing is the best practice.

Coaching is a very powerful way to support teachers as they strive to find ways to better meet the needs of their students. Integrating video into coaching increases the power of coaching in significant ways. Michelle Harris, who was one of the first coaches in our research cohort to use a camera, summed it up beautifully: "Coaching with video is like coaching on steroids."

> I think using video made my coaching more strategic. It's one thing to set a goal, write it down on paper, and talk about it. But having evidence on the video to show that there is growth and we're on track is powerful. We stay on the track to hit the goal.
>
> —**Christa Anderson**, Instructional Coach, Missoula, Montana

Turning Ideas Into Action

STUDENTS

Students can become a type of coach and be extremely helpful to a teacher as he pursues a goal for instructional improvement. Teachers can share their goal with students, explain why it is important, and ask students for suggestions on how to reach it. A teacher who is trying to increase authentic engagement, for example, might talk with students about the difference between authentic engagement and strategic compliance and ask students to suggest how he can make learning more authentically engaging.

TEACHERS

Coaches need to keep in mind that the video belongs to the teacher and that, therefore, the teacher decides everything related to the recording—where the camera is pointed, who sees the video (which may mean only the teacher views it), who does the recording, and what happens to the video after it has been reviewed.

COACHES

One way coaches can model the power of video is to use it to improve their own practices. Indeed, the coaches in our design study found that watching themselves on video was the most effective way to improve their practice. Coaches can ask their collaborating teachers for permission to video-record coaching sessions, explaining that the sole purpose is for the coach to improve practice. Recording conversations and reviewing the video afterward can be powerful learning. For example, I have recorded conversations with my wife Jenny and learned a great deal about how I communicate when I went back and reviewed the recording.

PRINCIPALS

In our interviews, teachers and coaches told us that teachers want to be reassured that their video is theirs alone. Thus, principals need to agree that teacher video will not be shared without teacher agreement and repeat that message until teachers believe that they and they alone determine what gets recorded and what happens to the recording.

SYSTEM LEADERS AND POLICY MAKERS

When budgets are tight, the positions of instructional coaches are sometimes considered the easiest to cut. However, if schools want to improve, cutting coaches is shortsighted. System leaders need to look carefully at budgets to determine how funds can be found to ensure that coaches are not viewed as an add-on luxury but a permanent way for schools to establish cultures of continuous improvement.

TO SUM UP

- Coaching using video is like coaching on steroids.
- Video captures the rich complexity of the classroom.

- Instructional coaches can use video to adapt solutions to the unique challenges and opportunities each teacher experiences.
- Use of video increases trust.
- Video turns the focus of coaching away from the coach's opinions and toward what matters—students' learning and teachers' instruction.
- Using video has implications for all components of coaching.
  - **Enroll.** Clarify that using video is a choice and that the teacher owns the video and, therefore, decides how it is recorded, who sees it, and what happens to the recording.
  - **Identify.** Use video to get a clear picture of reality and use video as a point of departure for setting a goal for coaching.
  - **Explain and Mediate and Model.** Consider sharing a video or videos of teachers implementing the practice to be learned.
  - **Observe.** Use the camera to record how a teacher implements a practice.
  - **Explore.** The coach and teacher should watch the video separately and then meet to determine if the goal has or has not been met and what the teacher's next action should be.

GOING DEEPER

In two previous books that discuss coaching, *Instructional Coaching* (Knight, 2007) and *Unmistakable Impact* (Knight, 2011), I have mentioned several books about coaching in schools, including Bloom, Castagna, Moir, and Warren's (2005) *Blended Coaching: Skills and Strategies to Support Principal Development*, Costa and Garmston's (2002) *Cognitive Coaching: A Foundation for Renaissance Schools*, Jane Kise's (2006) *Differentiated Coaching: A Framework for Helping Teachers Change*, Joellen Killion and Cindy Harrison's (2006) *Taking the Lead: New Roles for Teachers and School-Based Coaches*, Stephen G. Barkley's (2010) *Quality Teaching in a Culture of Coaching*, Nancy Love's (2009) *Using Data to Improve Learning for All: A Collaborative Inquiry Approach*, Lucy West and Fritz Staub's (2003) *Content-Focused Coaching: Transforming Mathematics Lessons*, Jan Miller Burkins's (2009) *Practical Literacy Coaching: A Collection of Tools to Support Your Work*, and Mary Catherine Moran's (2007) *Differentiated Literacy Coaching: Scaffolding for Student and Teacher Success*. Finally, *Coaching: Approaches and Perspectives* (Knight, 2008), which I edited, contains chapters by several coaching authors on many of the coaching approaches listed here.

Additionally, three books are especially useful in explaining the practices we see instructional coaches using:

- Atul Gawande's (2011) *The Checklist Manifesto: How to Get Things Right* explains the importance of precise explanations of practices.
- Chip and Dan Heath's (2010) *Switch: How to Change Things When Change Is Hard* provides, among other things, an excellent description of what is required to begin and change initiatives like coaching.
- Joseph Grenny, Kerry Patterson, David Maxfield, and Ron McMillan's (2013) *Influencer: The New Science of Leading Change* (2nd ed.) explains the importance of modeling as a part of change and learning.

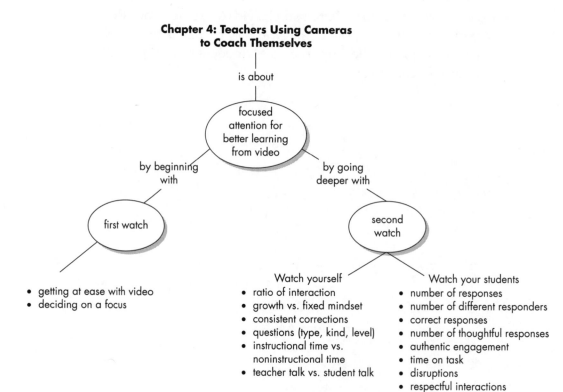

**Chapter 4: Teachers Using Cameras
to Coach Themselves**

is about

focused
attention for
better learning
from video

by beginning
with

by going
deeper with

first watch

second
watch

- getting at ease with video
- deciding on a focus

Watch yourself
- ratio of interaction
- growth vs. fixed mindset
- consistent corrections
- questions (type, kind, level)
- instructional time vs.
  noninstructional time
- teacher talk vs. student talk

Watch your students
- number of responses
- number of different responders
- correct responses
- number of thoughtful responses
- authentic engagement
- time on task
- disruptions
- respectful interactions

4

TEACHERS USING CAMERAS TO COACH THEMSELVES

Our acts of voluntary attending, as brief and fitful as they are, are nevertheless momentous and critical, determining us, as they do, to higher or lower destinies. The exercise of voluntary attention in the schoolroom must therefore be counted one of the most important points of training that take place there; and the first-rate teacher, by the keenness of the remoter interests which he is able to awaken, will provide abundant opportunities for its occurrence.

—William James, *Talks to Teachers*

What has been true for me (without exception) is that the problem I'm actually taping in order to solve always turns out to not be my problem at all. Something ELSE is my problem, and the video reveals that. It's like the device of the "MacGuffin" in Hitchcock movies—the thing the characters are after or searching for is not as important as what is revealed about the characters while on the hunt for that thing.

—Sharon Thomas, High School
English Teacher, Elkton, Maryland

In my younger days, I went on a hike with two friends in Jasper National Park in the Canadian Rockies. At one point, we stopped for a while at the base of a beautiful range of mountains on the continental divide in the Tonquin Valley and soaked up the spectacular view. After a few minutes, one friend, who spent all his spare time climbing mountains, said, "It's funny, whenever I see a view like this, I always look at the mountain to see the best route up to the top." My other friend, who worked on a trail crew clearing brush to create hiking paths in the park, laughed and said, "That's funny. Whenever I look at a valley like this, I look at the trees to see the best way to cut them down."

That conversation illustrates an important aspect of learning and experiences in general. We see what we look to see, and prior knowledge and intentional focus shape how we interpret what we see. When it comes to watching ourselves on video, this is good news because, if we are intentional about how we focus our attention, if we teach ourselves to focus our attention, we can learn a lot from what we see.

I learned about the power of focused attention while studying English literature, in particular John Keats. When I read Keats's poetry, I decided to supplement the experience by reading Walter Jackson Bate's (1979) wonderful biography of the poet. As it turned out, the more I read Bate, the more I saw in the poems. Bate's analysis of Keats's verse helped me know what to look for in order to appreciate the beauty of Keats's language. Bate's explanation that Keats wrote many of his great poems by the sea gave me insight into the imagery, and especially the rhythm, in Keats's poems. Bate's description of Keats's short life and his tragic experience with tuberculosis (he watched his brother die from the disease and then saw the same symptoms in himself before dying from it) deepened my insight into one of Keats's greatest themes—how beauty can help us transcend the impermanence of experience. Each bit of knowledge focused my attention and helped the poems come alive as I read them. In short, focused attention helped me see more.

A journalist once visited my family in Toronto. She spent the day walking the streets of the city, going from appointment to appointment conducting interviews for a story about theater in Toronto. When she came back to our house at the end of the day, I asked her what she had learned. "Well," she said, "I mostly learned a lot about shoes." Then she went on to explain that she had set out that morning wearing a new pair of shoes that turned out to be too tight. As the day progressed, her feet got more and more uncomfortable, and that pain caused her to look at everyone else's shoes. She suddenly noticed things about people's shoes that she had never before paid much attention to—they were worn out or unpolished, some looked very uncomfortable, some looked like bedroom slippers, and some shoes she wanted for herself. She learned all she did about shoes because the pain in her feet focused her attention. It's a shame that her article wasn't about shoes!

The point of these stories is that if teachers focus their attention, they can see and learn more about things around them. Teachers will gain a much deeper insight into the video recording of their lesson, as I did reading Keats, by focusing their attention on specific aspects of their teaching and their students' experiences. Watching a recording of a lesson with focused attention can be one of the most powerful forms of professional learning a teacher will ever experience. And it is easily done by employing a few simple strategies. This chapter details how to get the most out of watching a video for that purpose.

Video 4.1
Teachers Using
Video to Learn

*www.corwin.com/
focusonteaching*

Decide Where to Point the Camera

When teachers record their class, they should use whatever camera they have available, an iPhone or other smartphone, iPad, GoPro, Flip, or whatever they have on hand. Once they have a camera, the next step is to determine where they want to point it. Teachers may want to turn the camera toward their students or toward themselves. Teachers who are mostly interested in student engagement or behavior will likely want to point the camera at their students. Teachers who are interested in how they praise or correct students, ask questions, or use their instructional time may want to record themselves. Teachers who are especially ambitious may want to use two cameras and record their students and themselves at the same time.

Film a Class

Teachers will probably need to record at least 20 minutes of video. If they use an iPad, they simply fold the cover, prop up the device, and hit Record. They can also set whatever type of camera they are using against something, such as a stack of books, or use a tripod. Alternatively, they could ask a student to film the class (when they are sure it won't interfere with any student's learning) or ask another teacher or instructional coach to do the filming. When teachers use a GoPro with a fish-eye lens or attach a fish-eye lens to their smartphone, they just need to set the camera on a shelf.

After they record the video, they'll likely need to watch it at least twice—once to get used to seeing themselves on video and once to focus their attention on an aspect of teaching or learning taking place.

First Watch

The first time teachers watch their video, they need to keep at least two goals in mind. First, they should use the first watch to get used to seeing themselves on a screen. The first few times they see themselves on video, they may find it difficult to focus on their teaching and their students' learning. Most of us have had the experience of hearing our voice on a recording and being surprised at what we sound like. Seeing yourself on video can be like that—but to the power of 10.

Part of the problem is that most people don't like the way they look (including their clothes, voice, hair, movements). I have watched many people watch themselves on video and interviewed many people after they have had that experience, and so far, I have never heard anybody say, "You know what, I'm much younger and thinner than I realized." Video does seem to add 10 pounds and 10 years, and part of the first watch is just allowing teachers an opportunity to get comfortable seeing themselves.

A second goal of the first watch is to identify what teachers want to focus on when they watch the video for the second time. Watching a class can be overwhelming—do I watch the students and look at their level of engagement, their responses, or their behavior? Or do I watch myself to get a clearer picture of how I reinforce or correct students, how I deliver content, how I interact with students, or ask questions?

Clearly seeing and understanding all of these different variables at once is impossible. However, when teachers choose one area to watch carefully, they will see and learn a lot. After they choose an area of focus, they are ready to conduct the second watch.

Second Watch

During the second watch, the real learning happens as the teacher's focused attention reveals a clearer picture of what is happening in a classroom. When they watch the video the second time, teachers can choose to either watch themselves or watch their students. How to do that is described below.

WATCH YOURSELF

Reinforcing Students

Effective teachers encourage students by making sure students realize that they see them acting in ways that will help them learn. Teachers can learn a lot about the way they guide learning by watching how often they praise students for appropriate behavior and how often they correct students for inappropriate behavior. The ratio of times a teacher lets students know she sees them doing what they are supposed to be doing vs. the number of times a teacher corrects students is usually referred to as ratio of interaction (Reinke, Herman, & Sprick, 2011; Sprick, 2009) or positivity ratio.[1] For more information on ways to encourage students, see *High-Impact Instruction* (Knight, 2013).

A learning form such as the one in Figure 4.1 (all the forms in this chapter are available for download at the companion website, www.corwin.com/focusonteaching) may be used to record ratio of interaction, but you can also score the ratio on a blank piece of paper.

To score ratio of interaction, put a + on the paper every time you notice yourself reinforcing students with positive comments or nonverbal gestures and put a – on the paper whenever you see yourself correcting students. You may want to replay some parts of your video to be confident that you have coded the data correctly.

One way to think about ratio of interaction is to think of your attention as a flashlight. When you shine the flashlight—your attention—on a student because he or she is acting appropriately, record a plus on the paper. When you shine your flashlight—your attention—on a student who is acting inappropriately, put a minus on

> **What to Watch for When You Watch Yourself**
>
> - Ratio of interaction
> - Growth vs. fixed mindset
> - Consistent corrections
> - Interactions
>   - Opportunities to respond
>   - Type, kind, and level of questions
> - Instructional vs. noninstructional time
> - Teacher vs. student talk

---

[1]Randy Sprick and Wendy Reinke taught me about ratio of interaction and many forms of data collection when I collaborated with them to write *Coaching Classroom Management: Strategies and Tools for Administrators and Coaches* (Sprick, Knight, Reinke, Skyles, & Barnes, 2010).

| Figure 4.1 | Ratio of Interaction |

+	−

Ratio is _____ to _____

the paper. After you have watched the complete video thoroughly, add up your pluses and minuses and estimate your ratio of interaction. A general guideline is to strive for an average of five praises for every one correction.[2]

Possible goal: If your ratio is less than 5:1 and you think student behavior or learning might improve if you increase the number of positive interactions, you might want to set a goal to increase your ratio of interaction to 5:1 or higher. (Chapter 15, "Be a Witness to the Good," in *High-Impact Instruction* [Knight, 2013] contains many suggestions on how to increase the number of positive comments.)

> **Note:** Behavior that interrupts learning or violates norms or expectations has to be corrected, so trying to change ratio of interaction by decreasing corrections is not a good plan. The best strategy is to increase positive attention.

Growth vs. Fixed Mindset

In *Mindset: The New Psychology of Success* (2007), Carol Dweck writes about her research showing that people generally adopt one of two ways to approach the world: a growth mindset or a fixed mindset. If you have a fixed mindset, Dweck explains, you believe "that your qualities are carved in stone" (p. 6). If you have a growth mindset, on the other hand, you believe that "your basic qualities are things you can cultivate through your efforts" (p. 7). According to Dweck, people with growth mindsets are generally more successful than those with fixed mindsets.

With regard to teaching, Dweck found that the way teachers praise students can cause students to think in fixed or growth ways. Teachers, she says, should not praise students for being "smart" or "bright," since this encourages a fixed mindset. Instead, teachers should praise students for working hard, being persistent, or showing grit to encourage the development of a growth mindset (see Figure 4.2).

Teachers concerned with the quality of their praise can code how often their positive statements reinforce a fixed mindset: "You're so smart, gifted, awesome, amazing . . ." vs. a growth mindset: "You

---

[2]The 5:1 ratio is not a hard-and-fast rule. I suggest that ratio based on Gottman and Silver's (1999) research, which showed that a 5-to-1 ratio is typical in healthy relationships (*The Seven Principles for Making Marriage Work*).

Figure 4.2   Growth/Fixed Mindset Chart

	Growth	Fixed

clearly worked hard, your effort paid off, you've really demonstrated grit here, you are really showing progress thanks to your hard work . . ." A growth/fixed mindset form is available in Figure 4.2 to help teachers gather these data.

Possible goal: Teachers may set a goal to use only growth statements or strive for 90% growth statements.

Consistent Corrections

If teachers increase positive attention but fail to correct students, chances are they will not see students acting the way they hope to see them acting. Praising student behavior without correcting when appropriate is a bit like planting and watering a garden but not pulling the weeds. Eventually, the weeds take over. If teachers want to create a learner-friendly culture in their classrooms, they must correct students consistently.

When teachers issue corrections inconsistently (for example, allowing side conversations to go unchecked one day and correcting them the next), students become confused about what they can and cannot do, and, as a result, complain that their teacher is being unfair. In short, using corrections consistently is just as important as knowing what to correct, maybe even more important.

One thing teachers can observe, then, is how consistently they correct students. To develop the habit of correct corrections, they first need to clarify what behaviors need to be corrected. For example, they may want to correct students when they engage in side conversations, speak or act rudely, bother other students, move around the room when they are supposed to be in their seats, ridicule others, swear, or exhibit off-task or other disruptive behaviors. If the teacher and students have established norms, the teacher must consistently correct anyone who violates the norms; otherwise they will be norms in name only.

Teachers who observe their video for correct corrections are looking to see how often students should be corrected and how often they correct students when they act in such a way. To keep track of these data, teachers should note every time they see a correctible behavior and every time they correct the behavior. Educators may find it helpful to use the consistent corrections form in Figure 4.3. As a general rule, corrections should be consistent at least 90% of the time.

Possible goal: 90% correction of correctible behaviors.

Figure 4.3 Consistent Corrections Chart

	Observed	Corrected

$$\frac{\text{Corrected}}{\text{Observed}} = \underline{\hspace{2cm}} \%$$

Some teachers find it is useful to watch the video of their lesson once to identify what behaviors need to be corrected—by watching students. Then, once they have made their list of behaviors that must be corrected, they watch the video again to count how often students exhibited that behavior and how often they corrected or failed to correct behaviors.

Interactions

Opportunities to Respond. Another important variable teachers can watch for is how many times they give students opportunities to respond to what they are learning. This variable is meaningful only when teachers are engaged in what I refer to as intensive-explicit instruction—others used different terms, including direct instruction (Hattie, 2011; Roehler & Duffy, 1984), explicit instruction (Archer & Hughes, 2011), explicit, direct instruction (Hollingsworth & Ybarra, 2008), and strategic instruction (Ellis, Deshler, Lenz, Schumaker, & Clark, 1991).

During intensive-explicit instruction, as John Hattie (2008) has written about direct instruction, "the teacher decides learning intentions and success criteria, makes them transparent to students, demonstrates them by modeling, evaluates if they understand what they have been told by checking for understanding, and re-telling them what they have told by tying it together with closure" (p. 206).

Studies of intensive-explicit instruction recommend that teachers maintain engagement and confirm student learning by prompting students to respond at least four times per minute. Responses can include asking students to answer questions; prompting students to use checks for understanding such as whiteboards, response cards, or thumbs up, thumbs down (see pp. 62–65 in *High-Impact Instruction* [Knight, 2013] for a list of 19 checks for understanding); asking students to turn to their neighbor; or other forms or response. Offering a high number of opportunities to respond is likely not a good idea for teachers taking a constructivist approach to learning. (See pp. 12–16 in *High-Impact Instruction* [Knight, 2013] for more information on intensive-explicit and constructivist instruction.)

Gathering data on opportunities to respond (OTR) is quite simple: Just note the time at the start of your lesson, put a tally on a piece of paper every time you give students an opportunity to respond, note the time at the end of the lesson, count the number of OTRs, and then divide the number of OTRs by the number of minutes to determine OTRs per minute (see Figure 4.4).

Possible goal: An average of four opportunities to respond per minute.

Figure 4.4   Opportunities to Respond

$$\frac{\text{Total OTR}}{\text{minutes}} = \underline{\hspace{2cm}} / \text{minute}$$

Type, Kind, and Level of Questions. One of the easiest and most powerful adjustments that teachers can make is to reconsider the type, kind, and level of questions they ask. As I explain in *High-Impact Instruction* (Knight, 2013), it is important to choose the right questions for the kind of learning teachers wish to foster in the classroom.

- **Type.** Questions can be either open or closed. I define open questions as those that have an infinite number of responses. For example, if I ask you, "What do you think of Hemingway?" you might not say much or you might go on for hours. There is no limit to what you could say, and that is why this is called an open question.

  For closed questions, a finite number of responses are possible. For example, if I ask, "What was Hemingway's first novel?" there is only one answer—*The Sun Also Rises*. Some closed questions may produce lengthy responses such as, "What are all the novels Hemingway wrote?" but the essential characteristic of a closed question is that eventually you run out of answers.

- **Kind.** There are basically two types of questions: opinion or right/wrong. Opinion questions don't have a right or wrong answer. Opinions are personal and individual, so a person answering an opinion question can only answer it correctly, giving his opinion. For example, if I ask what you think of the Mango Chicken at Little Saigon, your answer cannot be wrong.

  Right or wrong questions, as the name suggests, have correct or incorrect answers. Teachers usually ask right or wrong questions to confirm whether students know the content or can demonstrate the skills they have been learning.

- **Level.** In many school districts around the world, teachers use Bloom's classification of educational goals, sorting questions into six levels—knowledge, comprehension, application, analysis, synthesis, and evaluation (Bloom, 1956). Others use taxonomies by Marzano, Erickson, or others.

  We have found it helpful to use a simpler method, which involves sorting questions into three categories: knowledge, skill, and big ideas. *Knowledge questions* prompt students to demonstrate that they can remember information. *Skill questions* prompt students to explain how to do something. *Big idea questions* prompt students to talk about the themes, concepts, ideas, and content structures that recur throughout a course.

Teachers can use the form in Figure 4.5 to assess the type, kind, and level of their questions. Generally speaking, for intensive-explicit instruction, teachers usually ask a lot (four per minute) of closed, right/wrong questions to confirm student understanding and ensure student engagement. For constructivist learning, teachers generally ask more open, opinion questions to prompt students to explore learning from their own perspective.

Possible goal: For constructivist instruction, 90% open, opinion questions.

Instructional vs. Noninstructional Time

During any period of instruction, there will be times when students are engaged in activities that promote learning (such as listening to direct instruction, cooperative learning, classroom discussion, reading, writing) and times when students will be doing things that do not directly lead to learning (transition activities such as settling in at the start of class, getting textbooks or other curriculum materials out, taking roll, lining up to leave class at the bell).

Obviously, the more students are engaged in learning activities, the more they will learn, so increasing the amount of time students are engaged in learning is a worthy goal. You can keep track of instructional and noninstructional time by using the stopwatch function on your smartphone (or use a stopwatch). Regardless of the tool used, the first step is to time each transition. Then subtract the total transition time from the total time of the class to see how much time was spent on learning activities (see Figure 4.6). For example, in a 45-minute class, if transition time was 15 minutes, then 30 minutes would be spent on learning activities.

Possible goal: Transition time less than 5%.

Teacher vs. Student Talk

One thing that surprises teachers when they watch their lessons is how much of the time they are doing the talking and how little of the time their students are talking about what they are learning. I am not aware of any clear guidelines for what percentage of time students and teachers should be talking; besides, the percentage would vary depending on what kind of learning is occurring. Each teacher, therefore, will need to make his or her judgment about how much talk is "enough."

Teachers can record teacher talk and student talk data in much the same way they record instructional and noninstructional time (see Figure 4.7). That is, the teacher notes the start and end of the class to

Figure 4.5   Question Chart

Question	Type	Kind	Level

Figure 4.6   Instructional vs. Noninstructional Time

Instructional	Noninstructional

Total Time _____   **Total Time** _____

Figure 4.7 Teacher vs. Student Talk

Teacher	Student

Total Time _____   **Total Time** _____

determine the total time, records when students are talking about learning, and subtracts student time from total time to determine the amount of time he talked.

Possible goal: As mentioned above, there is not clear evidence to support a specific percentage of teacher vs. student talk, but many educators strive for at least 50% student talk.

WATCH YOUR STUDENTS

If you choose to focus your attention on your students during the second watch of your video, there are many different data points you may want to monitor, including various focal points related to student responses, engagement, and behavior.

Responses

Number of Responses. As mentioned previously, during direct, intensive-explicit instruction, research suggests that students should make a large number of responses (at least four responses per minute). I discussed opportunities to respond (OTR) in the Watch Yourself section since teachers prompt opportunities to respond. However, OTR may also be the focus when you are watching your students.

Possible goal: As mentioned in the Watch Yourself section, an average of four opportunities to respond per minute is recommended in the literature.

Number of Different Responders. Achieving a high number of responses is not effective if the responses are all coming from the same three or four students. For this reason, when recording OTR, it is a good idea to also note who responded to prompts. This is easily done by putting a tally under a student's name each time he or she responds in some way. If the students respond to the same prompt, as in choral response, you can simply put a tally at the side of the page. Using a seating chart, you can record the total number of responses and the total number of different students responding.

One challenge is that teachers may not be able to see all the students on the video. However, if teachers listen carefully, they should be able to determine who responds to each prompt, or at least get a clear picture to see what is actually happening in the class.

Possible goal: At least 70% of students respond to at least one question during a lesson.

Number of Correct Answers. You can gain deeper insight into your students' responses by noting how many students give correct or incorrect answers, often referred to as correct academic responses. The right number of correct answers will vary depending on your instructional goals. For example, if students have 100% correct academic responses, that may be because they have learned the material, or it may be because the questions are too easy.

Students can learn much by making mistakes, so some incorrect responses can be a good thing. However, when students are giving many incorrect academic responses, likely some modifications to teaching are necessary. You can find suggestions on possible modifications to teaching in *High-Impact Instruction* (Knight, 2013, pp. 73–77).

To record the number of correct responses, using the seating chart for your class, put a + under a student's name when he or she gives a correct response and a – when the student gives an incorrect response.

Possible goal: Classroom management expert Wendy Reinke suggests that when students are learning new material, they should provide at least 80% correct academic responses. When students are reviewing content they have already learned, a reasonable goal is 90% correct responses (Reinke, Herman, & Sprick, 2011).

Number of Thoughtful Responses. The level of thinking students bring to any task may be observed in many ways. For example, you might want to use Bloom's taxonomy (Bloom, 1956) to look at how many student responses reflect one of Bloom's six levels of thinking: knowledge, comprehension, application, analysis, synthesis, or evaluation. Or you might want to use the levels of questions included in *High-Impact Instruction* (Knight, 2013)—knowledge, skills, and big ideas—or some other taxonomy of thinking.

One simple but powerful way of analyzing the thinking (or lack of thinking) underlying students' responses is to record whether a given response required original thought. If students are simply retelling what they see in a text, repeating others' responses, or merely guessing at what they think the teacher wants to hear, they are not demonstrating original thought. However, if students respond in a way that requires analysis, synthesis, creativity, or evaluation, then they are demonstrating original thought.

You can record the percentage of comments that involve original thought simply by drawing a line down the middle of a piece of note paper and designating one side as "Thought" and the other as "No thought." Then, as students respond, put a tally on the appropriate side of the paper.

Possible goal: At least 80% of responses involve original thought.

Doing It All

You can fairly easily record all of these forms of data while watching a video. First, use a seating chart for the class you are watching, code responses as + for correct and – for incorrect, and then circle the responses that involved original thought and leave the nonthinking responses alone. In this way, you can keep track of opportunities to respond, the number of different students responding, the number of correct academic responses, and the number of responses involving original thought.

Engagement

Phil Schlechty (2011) has identified three levels of engagement: authentic engagement, strategic compliant, and off task. When students are *authentically engaged,* they are doing a task because they find it inherently worthwhile, meaningful, or enjoyable. When the bell sounds to end a class, students who are authentically engaged would like to continue doing whatever they are doing.

When students are *strategically compliant,* they do a learning task because they have to do it, not because they want to do it. Students who are strategically compliant want to finish a task as quickly as possible so that they can spend their time on something that is authentically engaging.

Finally, students who are *off task* are not doing the task they have been asked to do by their teacher. They might be having side conversations, doing work for another class, texting, or looking out the window. Regardless of what they are doing, it is not what their teacher wanted them to do. You can learn a lot about student learning by observing students' level of engagement.

Authentic Engagement. The most valuable engagement data involve determining how many students are authentically engaged. A well-planned lesson that keeps all students engaged is one that should lead to learning. Unfortunately, it is hard to know just by watching whether a student is authentically engaged or strategically compliant. Any measure of authentic engagement, therefore, is fairly subjective. Nevertheless, much can be learned by watching students and estimating whether they are authentically engaged.

You can record authentic engagement using the document you would use for other forms of data gathering: a seating chart for the students in your video. There are many ways to record these data, some of which are discussed in *High-Impact Instruction* (Knight, 2013). One suggestion is to record engagement every 5 minutes during your lesson. To do this, watch your video for 5 minutes, pause the video, and then count how many students appear to be authentically engaged. Put a + on the seating chart under the name of every student who appears to be authentically engaged and a – under the name of every student who appears to not be authentically engaged. You may need to go back and forth on the video a few times as you focus on each student to determine whether he or she is authentically engaged. Once you have assessed each student, move your video recording ahead 5 minutes and repeat the process.

If, after viewing the video, you determine that students are not as engaged as you would like, review Part II of *High-Impact Instruction* (Knight, 2013) for teaching practices and learning structures you can use to increase engagement.

Possible goal: At least 80% of students are authentically engaged.

Time on Task. Teachers who are interested in a more objective measure of engagement could observe for time on task. When you measure time on task, you are measuring whether students are doing what they are expected to be doing; that is, are they doing the task they have been given to do? Stated differently, when you measure time on task, you don't distinguish whether students are authentically engaged or strategically engaged; you simply measure whether they are doing what they are supposed to be doing.

You can measure time on task in the way suggested for measuring authentic engagement—gathering data at 5-minute intervals. Additionally, as with authentic engagement, if you wish to increase students' time on task, you will find many teaching practices and learning structures designed to increase engagement in Part II of *High-Impact Instruction* (Knight, 2013).

Possible goal: At least 90% of students are authentically engaged.

Figure 4.8   Engagement Chart

Engagement Chart

Are you

| authentically engaged? | strategically compliant | not engaged? |

What could make this lesson more engaging?

Behavior

One advantage of using video is that you get a second chance to observe student behavior. Two items are especially helpful to consider: disruptions and respectful interactions.

Disruptions. When you are measuring disruptions, you are tallying each time a student disrupts another student's learning or your teaching. This is easy to do—just watch the video and put a tally on a piece of paper each time a student is disruptive. If two students are disruptive at the same time, score that as two disruptions. You can find many suggestions on how to reduce the number of disruptions in *High-Impact Instruction* (Knight, 2013), Part III: Community Building.

Possible goal: According to classroom management expert Randy Sprick, there should be no more than four disruptions every 10 minutes.

Respectful Interactions. Another easy-to-measure but important data focus is respectful interactions. Simply put, you are determining whether students are treating others in ways that are appropriate and acceptable in your classroom. Often this means they are *not* doing something—not shouting, swearing, touching, interrupting, and so forth. As with disruptions, watch the video and put a tally on a piece of paper each time a student says or does something that is not respectful. If two students are not respectful at the same time, score that as two disruptions.

Possible goal: Many teachers believe students should be respectful at all times.

The approaches for gathering data presented in this chapter are just suggestions. You may choose other methods. What matters is that you focus on something you think is important and observe it systematically. Then, after you watch the video, identify an area on which you would like focus your attention (increasing engagement, increasing correct academic responses, increasing your ratio of interaction) and set a goal, perhaps one of the possible goals listed in this chapter.

Once you have identified a goal, experiment by implementing various teaching practices, including those in *High-Impact Instruction* (Knight, 2013). Monitor your progress by recording and viewing more video, and keep at it until you hit your goal. Then, if time permits and you are ready, set another goal and go for it.

Turning Ideas Into Action

STUDENTS

When Cheektowaga middle school English teacher Lenette Braddock watched video of her class during the review cycle of her reading class, she saw clearly that students were not engaged in her lesson. To increase engagement, she asked the students for suggestions. Her students did not disappoint her. They told her they wanted to use their wireless chalkboards and write on chart paper using "stinky markers." They also said they loved candy. Lenette said she would not be giving them candy all day every day, but she did add a little incentive component to her lesson and gave out random prizes at the end of the week based on student work. She also added wireless chalkboards, chart paper, and markers as part of the lesson.

The result was dramatic. Students were much more engaged. By simply asking students for advice, Lenette learned a great deal about how to increase engagement and learning in her class.

TEACHERS

Video is a powerful way for teachers to get a clear picture of their teaching and their students' learning. In addition, it is a great way to monitor progress. Many teachers choose to keep early video recordings of their lessons so that they can clearly see how much they have progressed. Most people are encouraged and motivated when they see their progress vividly depicted in video recordings.

COACHES

Instructional coaches can benefit in at least two ways from the data-gathering methods discussed here. First, coaches can explain the various approaches to data collection to teachers and help them use them to deepen their understanding of their videos. Second, coaches can propose the variables as measures for goal setting with teachers.

PRINCIPALS

Perhaps the most important thing a principal can do to support teachers recording and watching their lessons is to clarify, again and again, that the video recorded in teachers' classrooms is the sole possession of the teacher who is recorded. Additionally, principals can encourage teachers to take the risk and use video by leading by example in using video to improve the way they lead meetings, workshops, or other forms of presentation or facilitation.

SYSTEM LEADERS AND POLICY MAKERS

As mentioned in earlier sections of this book, teachers' most pressing concern about using video is that it will consume a great deal of time. Policy makers should think carefully and creatively about finding ways for teachers to do this work. Additionally, teachers cannot do this work without technology, so schools should strive to have a camera in every wing and, ideally, in every classroom.

TO SUM UP

Teachers should watch their video at least twice: first to get used to seeing themselves on video and a second time to focus their attention on a variable that is important for increasing student learning. Suggested variables include the following.

WATCH YOURSELF FOR . . .

- Ratio of interaction, which is a way of assessing how you praise and correct students
- Growth vs. fixed mindset
- Consistency of corrections
- Questions (type, kind, level)
- Instructional time vs. noninstructional time
- Teacher talk vs. student talk

WATCH YOUR STUDENTS FOR . . .

- Number of responses
- Number of different responses
- Number of thoughtful responses
- Authentic engagement
- Time on task
- Disruptions
- Respectful interactions

GOING DEEPER

I was introduced to the power of gathering data as a part of coaching by Randy Sprick and Wendy Reinke. Specifically, Randy and Wendy taught me how to gather data on ratio of interaction, opportunities to respond, correct responses, time on task, and many other variables. Randy lists a library of excellent resources at his website, http://www.safeandcivilschools.com. All of Randy's books are extremely helpful, but teachers might benefit most from reading *CHAMPS: A Proactive and Positive Approach to Classroom Management*, 2nd edition (2009). *Motivational Interviewing for Effective Classroom Management: The Classroom Check-Up* (2011), which Wendy wrote with Keith Herman and Randy Sprick, is packed with valuable observation tools. In addition, it contains information on the importance of motivational interviewing to make change happen. In my opinion, motivational interviewing is one of the most powerful ways for coaches and other change agents to partner with teachers in coaching relationships.

The following books are also very relevant and helpful to the current discussion. Carol Dweck's (2006) *Mindset: The New Psychology of Success* summarizes her research on growth and fixed mindset. Martin Seligman's (2011) *Flourish: A New Understanding of Happiness and Well-Being* summarizes the research on positivity ratio and places that research in the broader context of positive psychology. Barbara Fredrickson (2009) summarizes her original research on positivity ratio in *Positivity: Top-Notch Research Reveals the 3 to 1 Ratio That Will Change Your Life*.

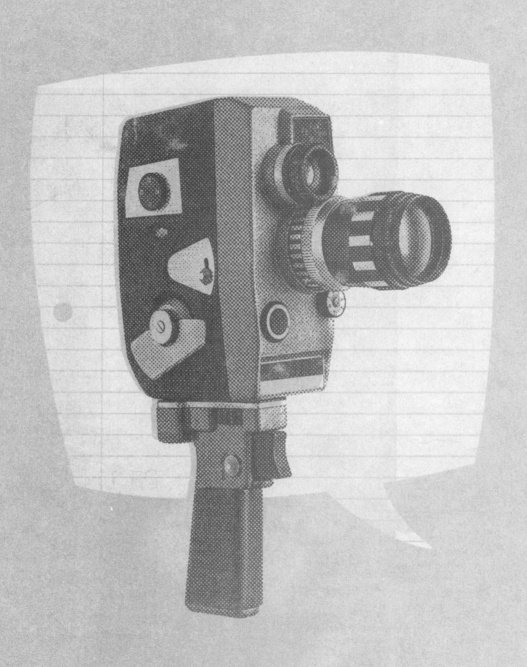

Chapter 5: Video Learning Teams (VLTs)

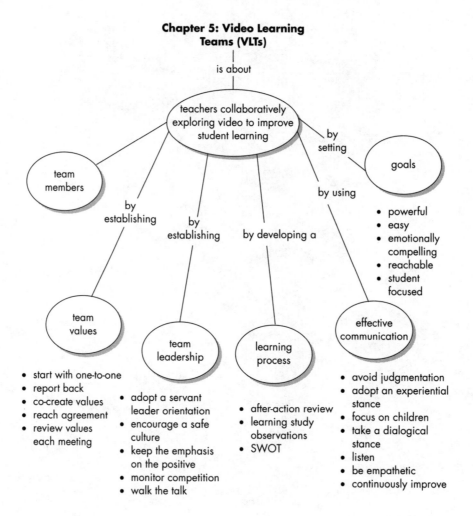

5

VIDEO LEARNING TEAMS (VLTS)

One of the big things you have to do is confront your reality. The next thing is you have to give up the dream of who you thought you were. That awareness is the beginning of all growth.

—Jean Clark, Instructional Coach, Cecil County, Maryland

I think that the bond that our team had stemmed from stripping everything away and starting over. We all wanted to get better. We put ourselves out there over and over again and talked through all that we do. And that was important to us.

—Michelle Harris, Instructional Coach, Beaverton, Oregon

"Human conversation," Margaret Wheatley (2002) wrote, "is the most ancient and easiest way to cultivate the conditions for change . . . If we can sit together and talk about what's important to us, we begin to come alive" (p. 3). In schools, teams can be the setting for such conversations, and video, I firmly believe, can be the catalyst that helps us "begin to come alive." "We humans," Wheatley wrote, "keep wanting to learn, to improve things, and to care about each other" (p. 8). Video learning teams (VLTs), properly structured, can be the place where such an authentic community flourishes.

Teams can use video to accelerate learning in many different ways. I discovered several approaches to VLTs when Marilyn Ruggles and I conducted interviews for this book. To paint a picture of how video can be employed within teams, I will start by describing three different approaches to team learning and then discuss strategies leaders can use to set up VLTs for success.

Team One: Coaches Improving Their Coaching. When Michelle Harris and her coaching colleagues first sat down with our research team to discuss coaching, she had no idea what might happen. As it turns out, Michelle's interactions with her team ended up producing a profound learning experience. But it wasn't easy. When I asked Michelle what it felt like the first time she watched herself on video with a team of people, she promptly and succinctly replied: "*Humbling* is the word that comes to mind."

Michelle, now an excellent administrator, was an excellent coach. When she joined our study, she had 5 years of experience coaching. She told me, "I felt like I knew what I was doing and that I kind of had it down. But when I watched the video with the other coaches, it became extremely clear to me that I was no model coach. It was mind-blowing! When I watched the video, I realized how many changes I needed to make."

The biggest issue Michelle realized when watching her interactions on the video was her need to focus on the teacher she was coaching—she needed to change the way she communicated.

> I didn't know what it looked like when I coached. If I had known, I certainly wouldn't have been shuffling papers, pretending I was listening when I wasn't, ignoring her [the teacher's] suggestions, and charging through and interrupting her—all the things I watched myself do on that video. I didn't know that's what it looked like when I was coaching.

As is often the case when professionals watch themselves on video, Michelle was overly critical of her practice. She is extremely accomplished, emotionally intelligent, and smart, and she has coached teachers to make very meaningful improvements in children's learning. In fact, I describe some of Michelle's coaching successes in *High-Impact Instruction* (2013). And yet, even this highly accomplished coach learned a great deal from participating in a VLT. Most important, Michelle decided that she needed to improve the way she listened.

> Listening was a big one. Truly listening. I thought I was listening. I was nodding and doing all the things you learn about listening from books and workshops. But I was just pretending

I was listening. I wasn't hearing anything she [the teacher] was saying. My body wasn't turned toward her completely. I was looking for what I needed to suggest instead of listening and letting her talk. I wasn't silent at all. I never shut up.

Michelle's decision to work on her listening is one of the most common communication goals people set after watching recordings of themselves. That is, out of the more than 100 people who watched themselves communicating as part of our global communication project, more than half identified listening as a skill they wanted to improve. Best of all, many of them, like Michelle, used their experience watching themselves on video as a catalyst for growing and learning.

Michelle told me that improving as a listener "didn't happen overnight. It was something that I really had to figure out how to do." But ultimately, learning to listen by watching herself, Michelle said, "changed the way I interact with people," and that change had a positive impact on her life:

I think that my career has taken off since then. The feedback that I get is that I do listen and that I do care and people do get that feeling from me. And I think that at home, too, I have learned to listen so much better to my husband, my kids, and my outside family.

Michelle's colleagues on her VLT were "instrumental" to her growth.

They were trusted colleagues, and I knew they were working on the same kind of things as I was. So to have them give me feedback was extremely helpful. That kind of feedback from colleagues who understand what you're doing and why you're doing it is essential. And you usually don't get that kind of feedback in education.

In addition to improving her communication skills, Michelle made important friendships with the other coaches on her learning team, Lea Molzcan, Jenny MacMillan, and Susan Leyden. "There is a bond that I share with everyone in that group that I don't share with anyone else," she said, adding,

Having video to review and talk about took everything deeper. You're talking about what you are doing as a person, and it's like therapy. We really hammered through some personal and philosophical thoughts. I know that if I ever, ever had some sort of conundrum or dilemma related to work I could call on any of these women and they would listen to me and try to help or coach me. We still get together every single month to catch up and talk about work.

The structure for the VLT meetings was simple. The team discussed each coach's progress on the components of coaching by answering four simple questions: What worked? What didn't work? What accounts for the difference? What should we do differently next time? Those questions, originally developed for U.S. Army After-Action Review,[1] became a conversation template for analyzing how coaching was working (see Figure 5.1), and through those conversations, the team refined goal setting, exploratory conversations, and other coaching skills. In fact, ultimately, they refined the way the coaches employed video as a part of the coaching process. What the coaches and our research team learned as a team contributed to the description of coaching I include in Chapter 3.

> I still crave that honest feedback— honest work around our work that you just don't get normally. There is no time for it; there is no space for it, or we don't make time for it, for whatever reason. That was truly the highlight of my professional career thus far.
>
> —**Michelle Harris**, Instructional Coach, Beaverton, Oregon

Team Two: Teachers Learning New Practices. Jean Clark, an educational leader from Cecil County, Maryland, has taught me a lot about how video can accelerate learning on teams. Jean, an instructional coach at Bohemia Manor Middle School in Cecil County when I first met her, believes deeply in the power of video. For Jean, "video is core because it forces people to go back and look at what they've done. Without video, we can't remember. We're bombarded with all these stimuli. We have to go back and see what we did."

Jean first realized how powerful video could be when she used it to help struggling students improve their communication skills. "I had a really difficult eighth-grade class, students who treated each other like crap. I started videotaping whenever we did any dialogue sessions because that was the time when they were most likely to come to blows." Jean was using the Touchstones Curriculum (http://www.touchstones.org). "The students," Jean said, "began to realize they had to collaborate with one another. I finally got them to the

---

[1]According to *The U.S. Army Leadership Field Manual* (2004), "An AAR is a professional discussion of an event, focused on performance standards, that allows participants to discover for themselves what happened, why it happened, and how to sustain strengths and improve on weaknesses" (p. 6).

Figure 5.1 After-Action Report

What was supposed to happen?

What happened?

What accounts for the difference?

What should be done differently next time?

Other comments? (Please use back of the form.)

leadership stage, and I got them there quicker than normal because I was using video. Video kept students honest, and it kept them engaged."

Jean then turned the camera on herself and her colleagues because she realized video could accelerate professional learning. She brought teachers together into teams so that they could watch and discuss video recordings of themselves using a specific instructional practice, *The Concept Mastery Routine* (Bulgren, Schumaker, & Deshler, 1993). This teaching practice involves a graphic organizer and instructional procedures teachers can use to ensure students master important concepts.

Jean established VLTs so that teachers could watch each other trying out the routine. Participation on the teams was not compulsory but was one of several options for professional learning offered to teachers on late-arrival days once a month in the school year. Only teachers who had chosen this learning experience participated.

Prior to each monthly meeting, one teacher volunteered to prepare and share a video for the next session. The volunteer recorded herself using the teaching routine in the classroom. After recording the class, the teacher loaded the video into iMovie and edited the film to find clips that depicted what she thought went well and what she wanted to improve. When they edited their films, volunteers had to watch their lesson many times, and those repeated viewings led them to see many details of their lessons that wouldn't have been obvious after just one viewing.

When the VLT met, the volunteer shared her video clips with the group, showing each section and asking for comments. At the very first meeting, Jean guided her team to collaborate and identify values they would work from while discussing each other's videos. They decided that comments about lessons should be positive, honest, constructive, and useful. "I think I went to video," Jean told me, "because I wanted everyone to have ongoing dialogue about what we are doing. That's the only way to change practices."

During the meetings, the volunteer usually shared two positive clips first. Then she talked about what she saw in the video clips and asked her colleagues for their insight into the lesson. During the final video, the volunteer asked questions as much as she commented. Eventually, each teacher in the VLT hosted a conversation about his or her lesson.

> It is painful to realize that what we thought is reality isn't reality, that who we thought we were is not who we are. That's a powerful realization that changes the direction of where we are going. This is very hard to do because you have to be vulnerable. But it's authentic. You have to say what you mean, and that's the way we become adults.
>
> —**Jean Clark**, Special Consultant, Cecil County, Maryland

Team Three: Teachers Improving Their Practice. At Red Hawk Elementary in Erie, Colorado, principal Cyrus Weinberger and clinical professor Rychie Rhodes are using video as a catalyst so teachers can have powerful and meaningful discussions about the way they are teaching. Each teacher on each grade-level team is video-recorded at some point in the school year, and an edited version of the recording of the lesson is used for discussion around teaching and learning during grade-level team meetings.

Cyrus and Rychie do a few simple things to make the teams work. At Red Hawk, when teachers agree to be part of a learning team, they agree to have 20 to 60 minutes of one of their lessons recorded. Cyrus and Rychie record the lesson and then edit the video down to about 15 to 17 minutes. Then they burn the edited video to a DVD and send the DVD to the appropriate grade-level team.

Each teacher on the team watches the video in preparation for the team discussion. While watching the video, they take notes using a template (see Figure 5.2) that focuses their attention on (a) the learning activity, (b) what the teacher is doing, (c) what students are doing, and (d) feedback they would like to provide. The use of video and the template, Rychie said, has led to practical, deep dialogue. "It is amazing how much more objective and richer the dialogue is after teachers have had time to think about the video."

Team conversations about the DVDs last from 45 minutes to an hour. The person who was video-recorded usually starts the conversation, but eventually other team members talk about what they see and have seen. The group works through the questions on the template, with Rychie taking notes on her iPad. At the end of the dialogue, the person who was video-recorded summarizes what he learned, and then the next volunteer explains how he or she will build on what has been learned. Everyone gets Rychie's notes about an hour after the meeting.

The staff at Red Hawk are very energetic about learning. They realize the importance of the teams, and they know the importance and value of this kind of dialogue. As a result, they have begun to share their teaching practices in a way that has not happened before. For example, Rychie explained that a team might watch the way a teacher and student interact and tell the teacher, "Wow, that really worked. I could see that student really light up." Then, Rychie said, the team might start to ask more questions, such as, "Do you do that daily? How do you keep track of progress? What's your management system for gathering data? Is it a weekly collection?"

Figure 5.2 Lesson Study Observation Questions

What is the learning activity?

What is the teacher doing?

What are students doing?

What feedback would you give this teacher? Strengths/next step(s):

Source: Created by Rychie Rhodes and Cyrus Weinberger, Red Hawk Elementary in Erie, Colorado.

This form is available for download at **www.corwin.com/focusonteaching**.

VLTs have led to "a lot of really rich aha moments." Teachers share ideas and learn how to implement what their colleagues are doing. For Rychie, perhaps the most important part of the team learning is how it promotes reflection. "During this rich dialogue, self-reflection is extremely important. During the meetings, teachers can talk about their reflection and reflect on how to implement new learning in their planning and then use it with their students. Reflection is an important step to get there."

VLTs have proven to be valuable for at least four important reasons. First, educators learn a great deal by watching themselves teach or coach, especially when watching themselves several times. Second, VLTs provide powerful follow-up to professional learning by increasing the likelihood and quality of implementation after workshops, since members of a VLT commit to implementing a practice and then explore different ways to use the practice by watching other teachers. Third, during the dialogue that occurs during VLTs, teachers learn powerful and often subtle teaching practices while watching others teach and listening to team members' comments. Finally, when teachers come together for such conversation, they form a meaningful bond, just as Michelle's team did, simply because the structure of a VLT compels them to stand vulnerably in front of their peers and engage in constructive, supportive, and appreciative conversations.

> By videotaping students as they are doing independent study, we are able to go to students and ask them what they are learning and why they are learning it. Having conversations with students is another powerful piece of this video lesson study. That's a formative assessment to take back to our debrief with teachers.
>
> —**Rychie Rhodes**, Clinical Professor, Red Hawk Elementary School, Erie, Colorado

Setting Up Video Learning Teams: Creating Psychologically Safe Environments

Amy Edmondson, mentioned in Chapter 2, has studied teams in corporations, hospitals, and government agencies, and she has found that teams need to be psychologically safe if they are to make an impact. In her book *Teaming: How Organizations Learn, Innovate, and Compete in the Knowledge Economy* (2012), Edmondson writes that in "psychologically safe environments, people are willing to offer ideas, questions, concerns. They are even willing to fail, and when they do, they learn" (p. 125). Edmondson includes a simple diagram (see Figure 5.3) that illustrates the importance of psychological safety and how it interacts with accountability.

Psychological safety is especially important when team members share video of themselves teaching because our identity is so

Figure 5.3   Psychological Safety and Accountability

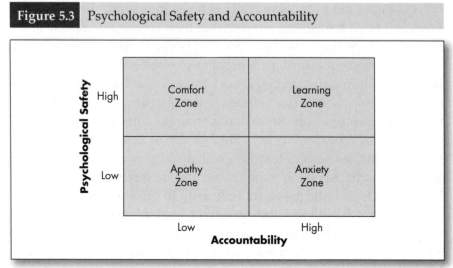

Source: Edmondson (2012)

interwoven with our professional practice. How we teach, truly, is part of who we are as persons, and that complicates interactions. Stone, Patton, and Heen (1999) highlighted three identity issues that seem particularly common and often underlie what concerns us most during difficult conversations: "Am I competent? Am I a good person? Am I worthy of love?" (p. 112).

For Stone and colleagues (1999), identity is "the story we tell ourselves about ourselves" (p. 112). Like many good narratives, our story can contain both fiction and nonfiction. Our identity is grounded in accurate and inaccurate assumptions that define us to ourselves. When those assumptions are proven to be false, it can be very difficult. Stone, Patton, and Heen (1999) write that an identity conversation can be "profoundly disturbing" (p. 112) and "cause you to relinquish a cherished aspect of how you see yourself. At its most profound, this can be a loss that requires mourning just as surely as the death of a loved one" (p. 114).

The emotional complexity most of us experience when watching ourselves on video involves much more than disappointment about our physical appearance or the way our clothes fit. Watching video of our practice brings us face to face with a clear picture of what we do, and that picture can threaten "the story we tell ourselves about ourselves." For that reason alone, asking teachers to watch themselves is very challenging. But asking them to watch themselves in front of their colleagues, ask for feedback, and give feedback to their colleagues, that's asking a lot more! This kind of conversation can take place only when there is a trusting relationship among the teachers watching the video.

Coming face to face with a new way of understanding "the story we tell ourselves about ourselves" can be very difficult. However, if we are to improve our practice, we need to get a clear picture of how we perform. VLTs are one setting in which this important learning can occur. Leaders who want to create psychologically safe environments for learning teams should consider following six suggestions, each of which will be explored further below.

1. ESTABLISH TEAM LEADERSHIP

Talking about a video recording of you teaching or someone else teaching is emotionally complex work. For that reason, it is important that a leader be identified to guide the team through the rewarding but complex interactions that surround learning from video. Such a leader could be a principal, instructional coach, teacher, or other educator. Leadership could also rotate on the team. Regardless of who leads the team, a few things need to be in place.

> **Creating Psychologically Safe VLTs**
>
> 1. Establish team leadership.
> 2. Select team members carefully.
> 3. Establish team values.
> 4. Develop a learning process.
> 5. Use effective communication strategies.
> 6. Set goals.

Adopt a Servant Leadership Orientation. When we think of leaders, we often think of powerful, charismatic personalities who take charge and make things happen. In settings like VLTs, however, the best leaders are not those who drive change through charisma and dominance but those who are most skilled at unleashing the potential in others. Robert Greenleaf in *Servant Leadership: A Journey Into the Nature of Legitimate Power and Greatness* (2002) identified this kind of leader as a servant leader:

> It begins with the natural feeling that one wants to serve, to serve first. Then conscious choice brings one to aspire to lead. That person is sharply different from one who is leader-first, perhaps because of the need to assume an unusual power drive or to acquire material possessions . . . The leader-first and the servant-first are two extreme types. Between them there are shadings and blends that are part of the infinite variety of human nature. (p. 27)

Effective leaders, Michael Fullan reminds us, are designers or architects who create an optimal culture and setting for learning. In *The Six Secrets of Change* (2008), Fullan writes that "Perhaps the best way to view leadership is as a task of architecting organizational

Video 5.1
Video Learning
Teams in Action

www.corwin.com/
focusonteaching

systems, teams, and cultures—as establishing the conditions and preconditions for others to succeed" (p. 118).

Leaders can position themselves as servant leaders by seeing themselves as partners with their colleagues. When leaders take this stance, they don't ignore the important responsibilities of leading, but they see themselves as equals with their peers. That is, they go into learning situations expecting to learn from their peers. When leaders are partners, they ensure that colleagues' autonomy is respected, they encourage dialogue between team members, and they ensure that team participants have choices, including whether to participate in a team.

Encourage a Safe Culture. To create a safe learning environment in which dialogue can flourish, team leaders need to monitor and shape the culture of the team. Effective leaders understand the personalities represented on their teams, and they intervene when necessary to ensure that conversation remains psychologically safe. Sometimes this means having to mediate conversations to build bridges between comments; at other times it means having to step in to ensure that everyone is free to speak and that comments are productive, not destructive.

Keep the Emphasis on the Positive. Marti Elford, a researcher colleague at the University of Kansas Coaching Project who spent 5 years as a member of our coaching team, told me that she felt it was critical that her team leader, Devona Dunekack, "always kept positive comments at the forefront." "Devona," Marti said, "began every meeting asking everyone to take 30 seconds to say something positive about what was happening at school." As a leader, Marti said, "Devona kept the emphasis on the positive, so we were affirmed and supported by each other, and that made it much easier to open up."

Monitor Competition. According to Michael Fullan (2010) and others, healthy competition can be good for a school or a team. Healthy competition occurs when team members push each other forward while also supporting each other. Healthy competitors work from an abundance mentality, assuming that everyone can succeed and that another's success is a good thing, not an indication that they are losing. In short, healthy competition is win-win.

Unhealthy competition arises when team members frown on their colleagues' successes and hoard knowledge and resources so that they will look better themselves. Unhealthy competition works from a scarcity mentality, assuming that only one person can succeed and that another's success is a bad thing because it indicates that I am losing. In short, unhealthy competition is win-lose. When unhealthy conversation surfaces, leaders need to intervene to keep it from interfering with learning or damaging team morale.

Walk the Talk. Team leaders also need to be sure to do what they suggest other team members do. For example, if a principal is a team leader, she needs to record herself teaching, even if this requires doing a model lesson in a teacher's classroom. The team leader must go through the same reflective activities as the other members of the team.

2. SELECT TEAM MEMBERS CAREFULLY

Teams may fall apart if they are put together carelessly. Talking about the way we teach requires psychological safety, so members on VLTs must to be committed to constructive, supportive conversation. An overly critical, defensive, negative, or self-centered team member can so severely damage the culture of a team that meaningful dialogue becomes impossible. As one educator told me, "You don't want to bare your soul to Debbie Downer."

One way to ensure that the right people are on the team is to make VLTs a choice rather than a compulsory form of learning. This was the case at Cecil County when Jean Clark established VLTs. The participants on her team freely chose the VLT learning experience, while other colleagues chose other formats for learning.

As I have emphasized in this book and other publications, professionals should have a lot of choice about what they learn and how they learn, in part because independent decision making is a defining characteristic of professionalism. At the same time, continuous improvement is an essential characteristic of professionalism. That is, while professionals should have a lot of choice about what and how they learn, choosing not to learn is unprofessional because, by definition, professionals continuously improve. As part of such continuous improvement, one important choice is whether to participate on a VLT.

One way that team leaders can explain the VLT process and clarify that the team is a choice is to meet with potential team members individually. During such a conversation, in addition to emphasizing that the team is important and powerful but not compulsory, team leaders can help potential team members better understand what will happen during VLTs, explaining how VLTs are structured, answering questions about VLTs, and asking potential team members what kind of team values they think should be established. Such feedback will be the point of departure for the first meeting.

Meeting one to one to establish team membership may seem like overkill, but after close to two decades of work in schools, I have found that one-to-one conversations are one of the most powerful strategies for leading change. In my experience, when people meet one to one, they are very honest and candid. However, when people meet in groups, they are sometimes guarded with their comments and shaped by an organization's cultural values. In addition, one-to-one conversations give team leaders an opportunity to deepen their connection with team members.

3. ESTABLISH TEAM VALUES

After team membership has been established, each team should identify team values,[2] the norms for behavior that everyone chooses as guidelines for how to interact on the team. In their classic book on professional learning communities, Richard DuFour and Robert Eacker (1998) write about the power of shared values:

> The most effective strategy for influencing and changing an organization's culture is simply to identify, articulate, model, promote, and protect shared values. When school personnel make a commitment to demonstrating certain attitudes and behaviors in order to advance the collective vision of what their schools might become, they are, in effect, describing what they hope will be the visible manifestation of their school's cultures. Furthermore, shared values provide personnel with guidelines for modeling their day-to-day decisions and actions. (p. 134)

To create a safe environment for learning before anyone ever shows a video from their classroom, team leaders should set aside time so that all participants can identify the team values they want for their VLT. As mentioned, this process begins during one-to-one conversations when each member is asked to describe the values that they think are important for a safe learning environment. Then when

---

[2]I have written more detailed strategies for establishing team values in Chapter 6 in *Unmistakable Impact* (2011).

the VLT first comes together, the team leader, while respecting the anonymity of members, can report generally what was heard during interviews.

As a next step, the team leader can move the conversation forward by asking a simple question: "What kind of team do you want to be?" As team members talk about the topic, all ideas are recorded on chart paper. The simple act of discussing values, which often addresses such issues as respect, listening, risk taking, encouraging diverse points of view, and caring for one another, gives each participant a chance to create the kind of culture they need to feel safe and ready to learn.

Before the next meeting, the team leader reviews the comments about team values on the chart paper and types them up in bullet form. (Repeated comments aren't typed again and again.) At the start of the second session, the leader shares the list of values and asks members to suggest what to add, remove, or modify.

Leaders should provide time for participants to rewrite the values every meeting until the group arrives at a fairly static document. Subsequently, the team leader can start each meeting by sharing the values statement with the group and asking, "Do we still agree with these values, or should we change anything?" This activity gives team members a chance to shape their team's culture, and the values remind everyone to act in a manner consistent with those values. See Figure 5.4.

4. DEVELOP A LEARNING PROCESS

One way to create a safe environment for a VLT is to establish a process for learning that members on the team understand before they start. In part, this involves certain nuts-and-bolts issues. For example, the team has to decide how much video will be shown, what kind of video will be shown (examples of effective or ineffective learning), who will speak when, what questions will be asked, and who will lead the discussion.

One way to structure the team learning is for the person showing a video of his or her teaching to host the discussion about the video. The team then follows a process each time someone shares a video, with each teacher/host showing a video clip, team members giving positive feedback, and the host asking specific questions to get ideas about how to address a particular issue.

Other formats are possible. For example, at the University of Kansas, our team agreed to use the After-Action Review, so collectively

Figure 5.4 Sample Team Values

Purpose: To develop and integrate a course sequence, teaching strategies, formative assessments, and lesson plans that help kids learn and enjoy mathematics.

Values

Respectful: We are honest; we listen carefully to each other, we demonstrate the courage to confront each other, and we resolve our conflicts constructively.

Efficient: We don't waste time.

Productive: We produce useful materials and tools that are teacher friendly and that help kids learn.

Supportive: We support each other and have fun together.

Validating: We value the expertise of everyone on the team.

Positive Thinking: We work together until we find solutions.

Consistent: We teach the same things, at the same time, in classrooms across the district.

Risk Taking: We are committed to implementing the materials developed by this group.

we responded to the same questions after viewing each video: What was supposed to happen? What happened? What accounts for the difference? What should we do differently next time?

In Cecil County, Jean prompted teachers to video-record their lessons, identify two parts that they liked and one part they weren't happy with, and then share those clips with their teams. At Red Hawk, an edited DVD of a lesson was created and shared with a grade-level team. Then everyone viewed the lesson using a template and eventually explored the following questions: What is the learning activity? What is the teacher doing? What are students doing? What feedback would you give this teacher? What are the next steps?

These teams often used templates or learning forms to enable learning. "Groups," as Bruce Wellman (2004) has written, "need templates to guide purposeful inquiry . . . collective focus is often difficult where there is no focus to the conversation" (p. 43). VLTs can get more out of watching video by using templates to focus their discussion.

In addition to the After-Action Review used at the Kansas Coaching Project and the Learning Study Observation Form used at Red Hawk Elementary, teams might also consider using a SWOT form such as the one included in Figure 5.5; more details about the process follow in Figure 5.6.

When teams use the SWOT template, specific guidelines need to be established for how to use it. Often, teams agree that the teacher in the video will identify or at least initiate conversation about the weaknesses and threats, with members collectively identifying strengths and opportunities and then, as a team, discuss ways to address the weaknesses and threats. My colleagues and I have used the SWOT template to discuss our presentation skills, and it has prompted a lot of powerful learning. However, the discussion prompted by the SWOT is direct and can be difficult to hear, so only teams that have a lot of psychological safety should use this template, especially at first.

One additional structure for VLTs is to employ an adapted version of the instructional rounds procedure described by City, Elmore, Fiarman, and Teitel in *Instructional Rounds in Education* (2009) and Troen and Boles in *The Power of Teacher Rounds* (2014). The process involves many of the components of high-functioning, high-impact teams as I've described them in this chapter.

Instructional rounds, City and her colleagues (2009) write, is "an adaptation and extension of the medical rounds model . . . [I]n the most commonly used versions, groups of medical interns, residents, and supervising or attending physicians visit patients, observe and

Figure 5.5 SWOT Form

	Helpful	*Harmful*

Teacher and Learning Structures

STRENGTHS

WEAKNESSES

OPPORTUNITIES

THREATS

Student

Figure 5.6 SWOT Learning Analysis

A completed SWOT form might include information such as the following:

Strengths. Characteristics/aspects of a teacher's methods or learning structures that increase learning.

- *Teacher Example:* A teacher's clear explanation of the rationale for learning increases student engagement.

- *Learning Structure Example:* The use of the think-pair-share cooperative learning structure made it easier for English language learners to find the words they needed to express their understanding of what they were learning.

Weaknesses. Characteristics/aspects of a teacher's methods or learning structures that decrease learning.

- *Teacher Example:* Tried to tackle too many outcomes and, as a result, students were unclear on what they were to learn.

- *Learning Structure Example:* Students didn't have the prerequisite skills to successfully complete the learning activity.

Opportunities. Student characteristics/interests that might be exploited to increase students' learning.

- *Example:* Students' interest in baseball provides an opportunity to teach statistics concepts through baseball statistics.

Threats. Student characteristics/interests that might interfere with their learning.

- *Example:* Students' learned helplessness about math means that they come to class expecting to fail.

discuss the evidence for diagnosis, and, after a thorough analysis of the evidence, discuss possible treatments" (p. 3).

Instructional rounds, according to Troen and Boles (2014), involve the following components:

1. Identifying a rounds facilitator who moves the rounds process forward, keeps participants on task, and reduces friction.

2. Establishing norms.

3. Identifying a problem of practice. For example, "Teachers do not regularly facilitate critical thinking among and between students to make the subject matter meaningful."

4. Identifying guiding questions for observations that flesh out the problem of practice. For example, "How can we . . . encourage all students to ask critical questions and consider diverse perspectives about subject matter?"

5. Identifying a host teacher for every round whose class will be observed.

6. Having the host teacher complete a Host Teacher Preparation Form (see Figure 5.7), which is shared with others so that they know the topic of a lesson, the context, and so forth so they can better observe the class.

7. Observing the class.

8. Debriefing the observation by exploring three focus areas: observations, wonderings, and learnings. (p. 14)

Video can be integrated into instructional rounds in many ways. For example, rather than having seven teachers observe one teacher in a classroom, possibly creating an artificial experience, host teachers can video-record their lessons, load them on to a video sharing site, such as the Teaching Channel (www.teachingchannel.org), and each member of the team can then view the recorded lesson rather than the live lessons.

A more powerful form of instructional rounds might be for video to be added, as Troen and Boles (2014) suggest. Thus, teachers would observe the actual lesson in the classroom, and the lesson would be recorded so all team members could view it afterward but prior to the debrief during the team meeting.

Finally, host teachers could bring tight focus to the discussion of their lessons by sharing specific aspects of the lesson and asking for

Figure 5.7   Host Teacher Preparation Form

To help focus the round, please fill out this form and e-mail to your rounds group.

Name: _____ *Date of Round:* _____

1. Review/explain problem of practice.

2. Provide context for the lesson.

    What is the task?

    What is your role as the teacher?

    What are the students going to be doing?

3. On what should the observers focus their attention?

4. To what extent should/would you like observers to interact with students?

Source: Troen & Boles (2014)

feedback. This approach would be very similar to what Jean Clark and her colleagues did in Cecil County when they discussed how to teach the concept mastery routine.

5. USE EFFECTIVE COMMUNICATION STRATEGIES

Since talking about teaching is personal and complex, especially when it involves video of our teaching, two barriers can arise that interfere with the effectiveness of any VLTs. In some situations, we may avoid talking about touchy topics for fear of upsetting our colleagues. Avoiding the truth, in this way, inhibits group learning, since a team cannot learn when team members don't know what others are really thinking. As Susan Scott has written in *Fierce Conversations: Achieving Success at Work and in Life, One Conversation at a Time* (2002):

> Many work teams as well as couples have a list of undiscussables, issues they avoid broaching at all costs in order to preserve a modicum of peace, to preserve the relationship. In reality, the relationship steadily deteriorates for lack of the very conversations they so carefully avoid. (p. 6)

However, the opposite—saying whatever is on our minds—can also inhibit learning. When people are blunt and careless with their comments, they can deeply offend the people who bravely share their videos. Careless, critical comments, therefore, can create defensiveness, resentment, anger, and even tears. Speaking the blunt truth isn't much help if it is demoralizing and destructive and may not even be heard. What we need to do is speak the truth in such a way that it can be heard.

Instructional coach Michelle Harris from Beaverton, Oregon, effectively summarizes why communicating clearly is so difficult and important:

> When you set yourself up for something like a Video Learning Team, you need to be open to everything that's being talked about. You're putting yourself in a position of growth, and growth can be scary; growth can be sweaty; and growth can be nerve-wracking. But growth is oh, so important. You should be willing to have a trusted group of colleagues say, "You know, Michelle, right there, did you see what you did right there?" I feel that if you are not willing to talk about what everybody sees on the video, you are not ready to be on a VLT.

To create an optimal setting for learning conversations, a team on which people say what they think and others hear what is said, requires that many of the practices described in this chapter and book be addressed. Briefly, learning teams will be more effective when values are established and followed, guidelines and procedures are implemented, learning templates are used, and the "right" team leader is in place. In addition, the simple strategies described next can dramatically increase the power of learning conversations on any VLT.

Avoid Judgmentalism. Harsh, negative comments are especially destructive to a team because they divide people rather than unify them. When one teacher belittles another teacher's practice—"How could you let those kids get so out of control?"—his pejorative judgment shows a lack of empathy, sets him up as superior and the other teacher as inferior, and consequently erodes trust. As Michael Fullan has written in *The Six Secrets of Change* (2008), there are serious dangers to "judgmentalism":

> One of the ways *not* to develop capacity is though criticism, punitive consequences, or what I more comprehensively call *judgmentalism*. Judgmentalism is not just seeing something as unacceptable or ineffective. It is that, but it is particularly harmful when it is accompanied by pejorative stigma, if you will excuse the redundancy. The advice here, especially for a new leader, is don't roll your eyes on day one when you see practice that is less than effective by your standards. Instead, invest in capacity building while suspending short-term judgment. (p. 58)

In *A Hidden Wholeness* (2004), Parker Palmer offers a concise and powerful suggestion that can help us control negative judgmentalism. We should commit, he suggests, "to act in every situation in ways that honor the soul" (p. 170).

Adopt an Experimental Stance. Another factor that interferes with conversation about teaching is that people tend to be overconfident about how easy it is to improve instruction in *another teacher's class*. Effectively teaching a group of students is one of the most complex acts a human being can perform, and simple or glib comments fail to recognize that complexity. Talking about teaching, like talking about parenting, is easy until you have to apply the suggestions to your own students/children.

Team members can promote learning conversations by acknowledging the complexity of teaching and offering suggestions tentatively. The truth is that no strategy works 100% of the time in every situation, so we are more helpful when we admit up front that our suggestions are guesses at best. When we propose strategies to be tried by a teacher, we can propose them as experiments, acknowledging that they may or may not work. Thus, rather than saying, "You should do this," we can say, "I wonder what would happen if you tried this."

Focus on Students. One finding from our research at the Kansas Coaching Project is that coaches and teachers accomplish more sustainable change when they develop student goals rather than teacher goals. A student goal might be that "80% of students' responses during classroom discussion show original thought." (A teacher goal might be, "I am going to integrate more technology into my lessons.") When teams focus on measurable changes in student achievement, behavior, or attitude, they will have more impact on students' lives.

Teams that focus on students often set common goals for improvements in student achievement or behavior. Thus, a team might decide that everyone will strive to increase student time on task to 95%. Such a goal establishes an objective standard for excellence that guides everyone's work. More important, the goal compels team members to keep striving for improvement until the goal is met in a way that makes a difference for children. If a team establishes a teacher goal to use graphic organizers more often, for example, they might hit the goal but never know whether the goal had any positive impact on students. I include more about team goals later in this chapter.

A focus on students also has the advantage of providing a third point for conversations between two or more teachers, turning attention away from individual teachers and toward student growth. A focus on students depersonalizes discussion and increases impact. Parker Palmer (2004) wrote about the power of this kind of conversation, which "represent[s] neither the voice of the facilitator nor the voice of the participant(s)" (*A Hidden Wholeness*, pp. 92–93). Further, a student goal, instructional coach Sarah Coons said, "really takes the pressure off teachers. They think, OK, it is not a goal I am setting for myself, but it is a goal to improve for my students. It's about students and helping them improve."

Take a Dialogical Stance. Dialogue, according to Bohm (1996), is "thinking together." Dialogue is a way of communicating whereby team members are equal, share ideas, and respect each other's ideas. Dialogue is a conversation in which the focus is learning rather than winning. Dialogue is not about convincing another to adopt our solution to a problem. Rather, it is everyone listening to all opinions so that the best solution can be uncovered.

In his short, wise book *On Dialogue* (1996), Bohm uncovers the etymology of the word "dialogue," explaining that the original Greek meaning of "logos" is "meaning" and that the original Greek meaning of "dia" is "through." Thus, "dialogue" is a form of communication in which meaning moves back and forth between and through people. Bohm explains:

> The picture or image that this derivation suggests is of a *stream of meaning* flowing among and through us and between us . . . out of which will emerge some new understanding. It's something new, which may not have been in the starting point at all. It's something creative. And this *shared meaning* is the "glue" or "cement" that holds people and societies together. (p. 1)

When teams take a dialogical stance, they self-monitor to ensure they are concerned with learning rather than winning. More than anything else, this involves each member believing that everyone has something to contribute to everyone's learning; that is, each member respects the other members of the team. William Isaacs describes respect in his book *Dialogue and the Art of Thinking Together* (1999):

> Respect is not a passive act. To respect someone is to look for the spring that feeds the pool of their experience . . . At its core, the act of respect invites us to see others as legitimate. We may not like what they do or say or think, but we cannot deny their legitimacy as beings. In Zulu, a South African language, the word *Sawu bona* is spoken when people greet one another and when they depart. It means "I see you." To the Zulus, being seen has more meaning than in Western cultures. It means that the person is in some real way brought more fully into existence by virtue of the fact that they are seen. (p. 111)

Listen. Some simple strategies can dramatically increase a team's effectiveness and, perhaps most important, team members' need to improve their listening skills. Listening improves learning because each member learns more when they listen and because stopping to listen provides others with a chance to speak up and share ideas. In short, we learn more when we let others speak and when we hear what is said.

As I wrote in *Unmistakable Impact* (2011), effective listening involves three strategies: (a) committing to respectfully hearing what others have to say, (b) letting others be the focus of the conversation at least for some of the conversation, and (c) pausing before we respond to any comment to consider whether what we are about to say will open up conversation or shut it down.

A fourth simple strategy can also dramatically improve how we communicate if the three strategies mentioned above are too difficult: Don't interrupt. When we interrupt, the tacit message is that we believe that what we have to say is more important than what the other person has to said. Interrupting keeps us from learning from others; besides, it makes us look like jerks!

Be Empathic. Empathy, which Jeremy Rifkin (2009) describes as "the mental process by which one person enters into another's being and comes to know how they feel and think" (*The Empathic Civilization*, p. 12), improves communication because our knowledge of others' thoughts, feelings, and experiences helps us better understand their messages. Additionally, when we understand others' perspectives, we are better able to shape our words so that others understand them.

Empathy also improves trust and builds bonds between team members. Well-known psychologist Carl Rogers explains the unifying power of empathy as follows:

> [W]hen a person realizes he has been deeply heard, his eyes moisten. I think in some real sense he is weeping for joy. It is as though he were saying, "Thank God, somebody heard me. Someone knows what it is like to be me." (from Rifken, *The Empathic Civilization*, 2009, p. 14)

Continuously Improve. On a VLT, the emphasis is on learning, but that learning will not happen as productively as we would like if the team members don't communicate effectively. Teams that wish to implement the strategies described here, therefore, should commit to continuously improving their team communication skills. Jean Clark talked about this when I interviewed her for this book:

We need profound growth in education, but we have been very content with just little teeny bits of growth. We have to figure out a way in which more people are engaged in significant change. But the heart of change can be painful and risky. You have to let go of a dream you have and sometimes accept a painful reality. When you start to change, you realize you and everyone around you bought into a bad set of goods. So you have to say what you mean and risk the wrath of others. You have to do that because change is so important.

One way to improve everyone's communication skills quickly is to adopt the strategy of a VLT—that is, video-record meetings. I suggest recording team meetings and sending a copy of the video to each member on the team. Team members can then assess their communication skills using an evaluation form such as the one presented in Figure 5.8 and set a goal for how they will improve their communication strategies during the next meeting. At the VLT, team members can start the meeting constructively and positively by sharing what their communication goal is for the upcoming meeting.

6. SET GOALS

Unfortunately, even when a team speaks the truth respectfully and honestly, there is no guarantee that the team will do anything that makes a positive change in students' lives. High-functioning teams can have enjoyable and pleasant conversations, but those conversations don't always lead to actions that make an impact. Elisa MacDonald (2013) writes about high-functioning, low-impact teams in her book *The Skillful Team Leader*:

High-functioning, low-impact is deceiving to the untrained eye because it is extremely productive, yet what it produces yields little to no measurable gains for student learning. The team is efficient. Members utilize all the tools necessary for a high-functioning team such as group agreements, roles, templates, and agendas. Their collaboration enables them to accomplish any task; however, the task on which they choose to collaborate has little to no impact on student learning. For example, the high-functioning, low-impact team might walk away with a better system for filing kids to lunch, a teacher coverage schedule for administering midterms, or even an instructionally related task such as an efficient way to collect homework, but the learning challenges students had when the team started collaborating remain. (p. 32)

Figure 5.8　Video Learning Team Self-Assessment Form

Video Learning Team Self-Assessment

Date:

After watching the video recording of today's learning meeting, please rate how close your communication skills were to your idea.

In the video-recorded meeting, I . . .	*Not Close*						*Right On*
Offered suggestions tentatively but honestly.	1	2	3	4	5	6	7
Encouraged my peers by acknowledging their successes.	1	2	3	4	5	6	7
Actively demonstrated empathy.	1	2	3	4	5	6	7
Focused on learning rather than winning.	1	2	3	4	5	6	7
Listened more than I talked.	1	2	3	4	5	6	7
Showed respect toward my peers.	1	2	3	4	5	6	7

My goal for next meeting:

VLTs that are truly high functioning *and* high impact need to focus on action rather than talk. Action begins with the team's values. That is, teams are more likely to make a difference when every member makes an explicit commitment to act to improve the quality of children's lives. This commitment may even be written into the team's values. Team leaders can encourage norms of action by explaining during one-to-one conversations why it is important that everyone commit to an action focus. Also, during one-to-one conversations, leaders could explain that a commitment to action is a requirement for joining the VLT.

Perhaps the most powerful way teams can commit to action is by setting goals. Often we speak of SMART goals, which are variously understood to be specific, measurable, attainable (or actionable/assignable), realistic (relevant), and timely (or time bound) (Doran, 1981).

I suggest that teams consider a different acronym, PEERS, which highlights a few additional factors that teams should consider when setting goals. Teams that create goals that address the PEERS factors will likely find that their goals will have more impact. Each of the factors is described below.

> **Effective Team Goals**
>
> - Powerful
> - Easy
> - Emotionally compelling
> - Reachable
> - Student focused

Powerful. VLTs that want to make an important difference in students' lives should sort through every possible goal by asking a simple question: Will this goal make a real difference in students' lives? Thus, a team might list several possible goals, such as increasing student time on task to 95%, increasing students' vocabulary quiz scores to a 90% or higher average, decreasing student disruptions to fewer than 4 per 10 minutes, improving the quality of students' writing, and so forth. The team should then use the impact form in Figure 5.9 to determine which goal will have the most impact on student achievement. Being powerful, however, is only one characteristic of high-leverage goals.

Easy. Powerful goals that are difficult or impossible to implement are not as helpful as powerful goals that are easy to implement. Difficult-to-implement goals, no matter how powerful, often end up on the scrap heap of unrealized good intentions. The best goals are goals that are powerful and easy, because they have the greatest likelihood of being implemented, and because they provide more time for teachers, who are very busy, to work on other important tasks.

Figure 5.9 Impact Goal Form

Impact Goal

Date:

After listing all of your possible goals, use the following form to identify the goal that has the greatest potential for impact. Complete one form for each potential goal. The goal with the highest score is usually the best.

	Not Close						*Right On*
This potential goal is . . .							
Powerful.	1	2	3	4	5	6	7
Easy.	1	2	3	4	5	6	7
Emotionally compelling.	1	2	3	4	5	6	7
Reachable.	1	2	3	4	5	6	7
Student focused.	1	2	3	4	5	6	7

Comments:

In *Influencer: The Power to Change Anything* (2008), Patterson and his colleagues explain why easy and powerful goals are so important:

> When it comes to altering behavior, you need to help others answer only two questions. First: Is it worth it? . . . And second: Can they do this thing? . . . Consequently, when trying to change behaviors, think of the only two questions that matter. Is it worth it? . . . Can I do it? (p. 50)

Emotionally Compelling. In their book *Switch: How to Change Things When Change Is Hard* (2010), Heath and Heath suggest that effective goals need to be more than SMART; they need to compel people to action by moving them emotionally. According to the authors, effective goals "provide a destination postcard—a vivid picture from the near-term future that shows what could be possible" (p. 76).

To illustrate the power of emotionally compelling goals, Heath and Heath (2010) compare two reading goals for a kindergarten class. The first, the authors say, is "a way not to do it":

> With respect to reading for the school year, I administered three diagnostics: WWT, Assessments of Comprehension, and Monster Test. Using CWT, I identified my classes' average as grade level 1.5 in September. My goal is to increase my classes' word identification so as to ensure a class average of 3.0. Upon analyzing the results of the Assessment of Comprehension, I identified my classes' average as a 41% in September. My goal is to increase my students' comprehension so as to ensure a class average of 80%. Using the Monster Test, I identified my classes' average score as Semiphonetic/Phonetic. My goal is to increase my students' phonics and spelling skills to Transitional. (p. 74)

Such a goal, the authors write, might help the teacher with her planning, but it won't "light . . . a fire in the hearts of the first graders." In contrast, the authors describe an emotionally compelling goal created by a teacher of a first-grade class in Atlanta, Georgia:

> Crystal Jones . . . knew if she wanted to motivate the kids she had to speak their language. At the beginning of the school year, she announced a goal for her class that she knew would captivate every student: By the end of this school year you're going to be *third graders* . . . That goal was tailor-made for the first-grade psyche. First graders know very well what third

graders look like—they are bigger, smarter, and cooler. You know the feeling you get when you're admiring the grace and power of an Olympic athlete? That's the feeling first graders get about third graders. (Heath & Heath, 2010, pp. 74–75)

Crystal Jones' goal worked because it moved her students to action. Her goal "was inspirational. It tapped into feeling . . . [it] 'hit you in the gut'" (p. 76). And it worked. "By the end of the year, over 90% of the kids were reading at or above a third-grade level" (Heath & Heath, 2010, p. 75).

Reachable. Few things are more unifying for teams than achieving important goals together. Not achieving goals can have the opposite impact and damage team morale. For that reason, teams need to consider whether their goal, however admirable, is one that can actually be reached. A reachable goal is one that builds hope.

Shane Lopez, a researcher at the University of Kansas and the Gallup Organization, has been described as the world's leading expert on hope. In *Making Hope Happen: Create the Future You Want for Yourself and Others* (2013), Lopez writes that hope requires three elements. First, hope requires a goal that sets out an idea of "where we want to go, what we want to accomplish, who we want to be" (p. 24). Second, to feel hope, we need agency, our "perceived ability to shape our lives day to day . . . [our knowledge that] . . . we can make things happen" (p. 25). Finally, hope requires pathways, "plans that carry us forward" (p. 25).

Shane Lopez's Elements of Hope

- Goals
- Agency
- Pathways

A goal that fosters hope is a goal that has a reasonable chance of being achieved because (a) team members believe they can achieve it (agency) and (b) it includes a strategy or strategies that can help them achieve it (pathways). Increasing student achievement by 20% on the state reading assessment is an admirable goal, but it isn't helpful unless the team can identify a strategy that will help them reach the goal. Decreasing noninstructional time from 22% to 5% by teaching students expectations for transitions, for example, is a more effective goal because it shows the destination as well as the pathways that teachers can realistically expect will get them there.

A reachable goal also has to be one that people will know they have reached. That is, as SMART goals have shown for years, the goal has to be measurable. Having students read more effectively is not a measurable goal, but having students read as well as third-grade students is one that teachers can know they have reached.

Student Focused. Finally, as we have found with our research on coaching, and as mentioned in Chapter 3, effective goals are student rather than teacher focused. When teams choose teacher goals ("Let's use graphic organizers at least twice a week"), they may implement the goal but have no idea whether it made a difference for students. Additionally, no measure of excellence is built into the goal, so people may implement the goal poorly and still meet the goal.

A student-focused goal, on the other hand, provides clear feedback on whether changes make a difference for students. Additionally, student-focused goals carry with them a built-in measure of quality. If a teacher ineffectively implements the teaching practice the team has chosen, it is unlikely that he will achieve the goal. The teacher will have to keep refining his use of the practice until he is able to implement it effectively, so that its use can lead to achievement of the goal. Often, an instructional coach is invaluable as a support for this kind of professional learning.

Turning Ideas Into Action

STUDENTS

Students' voices can help VLTs stay grounded and focused on student growth when students are a part of VLT work. This can happen in many ways. For example, students can be video-interviewed in a class or outside of class on topics such as motivation, school culture, school learning, obstacles to learning, school relevance, and so on. Video-recording students while asking them to describe their most valuable learning experience and then sharing those interviews during VLTs can be very enlightening. Interviews may be conducted by teachers, instructional coaches, principals, or students. Another suggestion is to invite students to VLTs and get their insights into videos of lessons. Students likely will have important thoughts to share about what it means to be a learner.

TEACHERS

Teachers' most important contribution is to commit to the VLT process. A team will not have any impact on students unless each member commits to improving practice for students. This means that team members commit to at least experimenting with the entire VLT process, video-recording themselves, watching the video, setting goals, and learning strategies to achieve the goals. Teachers can

(Continued)

(Continued)

also contribute to the greater good of the school by sharing their experiences on the VLT with other teachers and encouraging them to participate in their own VLT.

COACHES

Coaches can be extremely helpful in making VLTs work. First, coaches can lead VLTs, supporting teachers as they learn how to use technology, establish team values, and learn the VLT process. Second, since instructional coaches usually have a deep understanding of instructional practices, they can help teams by suggesting practices they might adopt in order to reach a goal. Finally, once a team has picked a strategy, an instructional coach can help the team implement it by meeting to explain, model, observe, and explore (see Chapter 3 for more information) the practice as it is learned and refined. Instructional coaches should also consider using the PEERS approach to goal setting during one-to-one coaching.

PRINCIPALS

Like coaches, principals can also lead VLTs or participate in VLTs led by instructional coaches or teachers. As leaders, principals must be careful to embrace the servant leadership approach. As participants, principals must be full partners in the process, video-recording themselves and following the team processes and values. Most important, perhaps, principals must ensure that VLTs are led in a way that will work, with team leaders, processes, values, and so forth. When teams are left to fend for themselves without support, there is a strong likelihood that they will encounter crippling roadblocks that keep them from being effective.

SYSTEM LEADERS AND POLICY MAKERS

District leaders can help make VLTs a reality by striving to find funds that will give teachers time to meet. VLTs that are added on to an already packed day—meetings from 6:45 to 7:30 a.m., for example—are hard to sustain. Leaders should try to do everything they can to make it easier for teachers to meet, watch video, identify strategies, and implement those strategies to make a difference for children. Leaders should consider reading DuFour and Fullan's *Cultures Built to Last: Systemic PLCs at Work* (2013) to get insight into how they can better support teams and coaches in their system.

TO SUM UP

VLTs are more successful when the following issues are addressed:

- Team participants should feel psychologically safe, since watching video can lead us to question our assumptions about ourselves.
- Team leaders should carefully pick team members to ensure a psychologically safe environment.
- Participation in a VLT should be voluntary.
- Team members should establish team values.
- Someone (often an instructional coach or principal) should be identified to lead the team by adopting a servant leadership approach.
- Teams need to adopt a clear, effective process for learning that often involves the use of templates that promote reflection.
- Team members need to use communication skills that allow them to speak the truth in a way that can be heard.
- Teams should set goals that are powerful, easy, emotionally compelling, reachable, and student focused.

GOING DEEPER

Rick DuFour and his colleagues have created a library of helpful resources for popularizing and explaining effective teams, referred to as professional learning communities (PLCs). DuFour's classic work, *Professional Learning Communities at Work: Best Practices for Enhancing Student Achievement* (1998, with R. E. Eaker), provides a great introduction to PLCs, but all of his books will help you create a positive, effective learning team. In addition, Rick DuFour and Michael Fullan's *Cultures Built to Last: Systemic PLCs at Work* (2013) deals with how PLCs (and, I think, any approach to learning, such as instructional coaching) can be successfully supported with a system.

Elisa MacDonald's *The Skillful Team Leader: A Resource for Overcoming Hurdles to Professional Learning for Student Achievement* (2013) is a sophisticated but accessible manual on how to create and lead high-functioning, high-impact teams. In addition, Bruce Wellman has written or co-authored many books that would benefit teams and coaches. In particular, his *Data-Driven Dialogue: A Facilitator's Guide to Collaborative Inquiry* (2004) greatly influenced my thinking about using templates during the discussion of video.

My favorite communication book, and I have read many, is Margaret Wheatley's *Turning to One Another: Simple Conversations to Restore Hope to the Future* (2009). This book beautifully makes the point that respectful, deep communication is essential for a life filled with love, learning, and hope. In every book I write, I also mention Stone, Patton, and Heen's *Difficult Conversations: How to Discuss What Matters* (2010) because those authors do such a great job of describing how our identity interferes with our ability to communicate and learn. Parker Palmer's *The Courage to Teach: Exploring the Inner Landscape of a Teacher's Life* (2007) is my favorite book about teaching. I especially like his description of how who we are is intimately a part of what and how we teach.

Finally, Heidi Grant Halvorson's concise book *9 Things Successful People Do Differently* (2011) is the best summary of goal setting that I have read. Heath and Heath's *Switch: How to Change Things When Change Is Hard* (2010) explains why goals need to be emotionally compelling and a lot more about leading change.

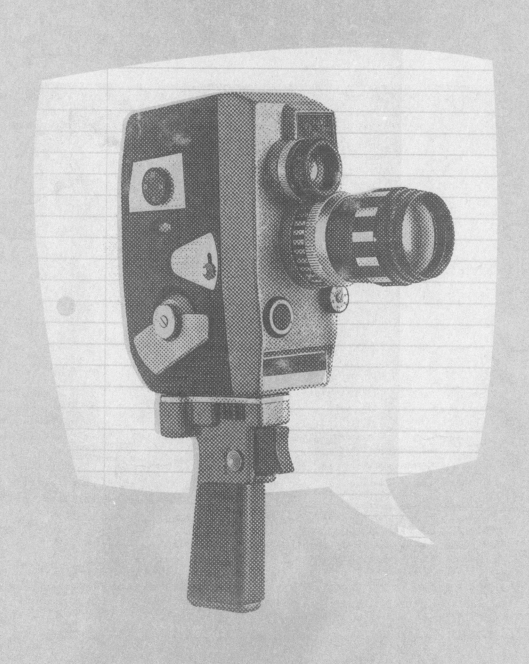

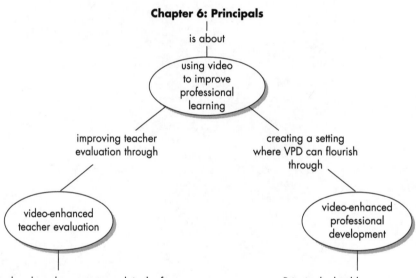

Chapter 6: Principals

is about

using video to improve professional learning

improving teacher evaluation through

creating a setting where VPD can flourish through

video-enhanced teacher evaluation

video-enhanced professional development

1. Principal and teacher meet to explain the form.
2. Principal observes and records lesson.
3. Principal and teacher watch video separately.
4. Principal and teacher discuss what they saw.

Principals should
- walk the talk
- shape culture
- fight for resources
- develop deep knowledge
- employ partnership leadership

6

PRINCIPALS

Having the video as a snapshot in time of what actually happened in the classroom gave us a discussion that was rooted in the "real" as opposed to what I think I may have experienced. Our conversation starts from the same place—this is what we saw on tape.

—Chad Harnisch, Principal, Rice Lake, Wisconsin

When Chad Harnisch looked ahead to his duties as principal at Rice Lake High School in Wisconsin, he wasn't especially happy about having to complete 60 teacher evaluations. "I hated it," he said. "Years ago, I heard some advice that made a lot of sense to me: Do the minimum number of evaluations required by the contract and spend the rest of the time having professional conversations with teachers about student growth."

Chad is a dedicated professional, deeply committed to achieving the best for the students and adults in his school. The reason he hated "the management task of having to complete 60 evaluations" was that, as far as he could see, it was "nothing more than that—a management task." Chad elaborated on his thinking:

The discussion is only about perceptions; my perceptions as a principal and her perceptions as a teacher, going back and forth between those two positions, trying to come to some negotiated middle ground about what happened.

What happens is that I do an observation in a class and take notes, but I don't have an opportunity to summarize notes right away—it can be two, three days, and sometimes as long as a week, before I get to sit down to do the actual evaluation. I don't have perfect recall, so when I write it, I know it's not perfect because it is based on my memory of what I think happened as opposed to what actually happened.

The evaluation conversation "was not effective professional development, and it was not coaching in the way that I would want it to be," Chad continued. "The conversation always has an element of confrontation because the teacher is remembering what she thinks happened from her perspective, and I am remembering what I think happened from my perspective, and there can be a disconnect between those two remembrances."

When talking about evaluation, principal and teacher simply attempt to arrive at a compromise decision about what really happened. But Chad wanted to find a way to make teacher evaluation something that actually made a difference for students and teachers. He decided to use video.

Chad met with one of his teachers, Amy Pelle, an "amazing professional," whom he described as "maybe the best teacher I have worked with," and asked her if she would try an experiment that involved video-recording her class as a part of teacher evaluation. Chad knew Amy wasn't interested in professional learning unless it had practical application, so he proposed they integrate video into the teacher-evaluation process. "I was curious about how critical Amy would be about her teaching as well as her reflections when talking about video." But Chad was most interested in what would happen when his conversations with the teacher were based on "what really happened in the classroom rather than what you think you remember happening in the classroom."

Chad and Amy decided they would focus their attention on the instruction domain of Danielson's framework (Danielson, 2007). First, they went over the assessment tool together and agreed on how to use it to analyze what was recorded on video. Then Chad used his iPad to video-record a lesson.

During the class Amy chose for recording, her students were doing independent practice, and Amy circled around the room working with individual students. While recording the class, Chad moved the camera as Amy moved around. Since he used his iPad in the classroom to do walkthroughs, the students were "used to seeing it in his hands, so they didn't even notice the camera." After the class, he shared the video with Amy through Google Docs.

Chad and Amy watched the video and completed the evaluation form separately before meeting twice. The first time, Chad said, they met "just to talk through our evaluation and how we ended up making our notations on the form." Chad gave Amy a copy of *High-Impact Instruction* (Knight, 2013) and asked her to read it before they met a second time to talk about more specific goals for teaching. That conversation turned out to be totally different from any Chad had ever had about evaluation. "The conversation we had was much more rooted in the *real* as opposed to being rooted in *this is what I think I have experienced*."

> The video gave us a snapshot in time of what actually happened and provided a discussion point that wasn't theoretical. It was about *this is what actually happened*, not *what I saw*, not *what I experienced*, but *what actually happened*. What the video did was to eliminate the conversation about our different remembrances, and instead of that disconnect we had an indisputable this-is-what-happened moment. So, our conversation started from a place of commonality as opposed to a position of diversion. The video is what really happened. We were talking about what was on the video right in front of us, and that allowed the conversation to be a much more focused conversation about teaching and learning.

Chad further commented that he "couldn't believe the difference in the conversation" he had with Amy after they watched the recording, explaining,

> If I had gone in and done it the old way—just gone in with the form and then later marked down my evaluation—it would have been "distinguished, distinguished, distinguished." It still was that after watching the video, but the video allowed us to have specific things to talk about. It allowed us to have a more professionally rich conversation. I'm going to offer it to all the teachers.

Principals lead the way when video is introduced in a school, and as with any initiative, their actions can make or break it. To foster widespread productive use of video, principals must play at least two essential roles. First, as the primary evaluator of teachers, they can, as Chad Harnisch did, dramatically increase the power of conversations about teacher evaluation by making video an optional part of teacher evaluation—I call this video-enhanced teacher evaluation. Second, as the principal leader in the school, principals can help create settings in which teachers, coaches, and teams can all successfully implement VPD. Both of these roles are critical, and both are discussed below.

Video-Enhanced Teacher Evaluation

Principals today are evaluating teachers more than ever before (Popham, 2013). Principals dedicate enormous amounts of time and worry to teacher observations, but unfortunately, the truth is that despite all these efforts, teacher observations may have no impact on teaching. In worst-case scenarios, teacher observations and evaluations make things worse rather than better by decreasing teacher morale.

The sad state of teacher observation and evaluation is summed up by the words of a young principal I met during a Texas workshop: "If the teacher doesn't cry or get angry," he said, "I feel the evaluation conversation has been a good one."

Video can dramatically improve the impact of teacher evaluation. Video-enhanced professional learning changes teacher evaluation from being a task to be endured to becoming a powerful reflective conversation that ultimately leads to improved student learning.

A simple four-part process for video-enhanced teacher evaluation can solve these problems efficiently. First, the principal meets with a volunteer teacher and explains the observation system. Second, the principal observes the teacher's class and video-records a lesson. Third, the principal and teacher watch the video and complete the observation system. Finally, the principal and teacher get together to compare and contrast what they found when they conducted the observation. Each of these parts of the process is described in more detail.

> **Video-Enhanced Teacher Evaluation**
>
> 1. Principal meets with teacher and explains the observation form.
>
> 2. Principal observes and video-records a lesson.
>
> 3. Principal and teacher watch the video and complete the observation form.
>
> 4. Principal and teacher meet to discuss what they found.

Determining Who Participates. As I've stressed throughout this book, I do not feel that teachers should be forced to participate in video learning teams (VLTs). This also applies to video-enhanced teacher evaluation. Telling people they have to participate in video-enhanced teacher evaluation will likely increase resentment more than learning. My advice is that video be an alternative that teachers can choose if they wish. Principals can explain to teachers that any video recordings will be seen only by the participating teacher and the principal and that the goal behind videotaping is to ensure that they have a meaningful conversation about what happened during the lesson.

Meeting to Discuss the Observation Framework. Most schools have adopted some kind of observation form or process. Many schools utilize Charlotte Danielson's *Enhancing Professional Practice: Framework for Teaching* (2007). Others use the 20-minute high-impact survey included in *High-Impact Instruction* (Knight, 2013),[1] the Marzano Teacher Evaluation Model (http://www.marzanocenter.com), or some other framework. Whatever observation tool or framework is being used, for video-enhanced teacher evaluation to work, both principal and teacher need to understand the evaluation tool.

To ensure that everyone understands the evaluation tool, principals and teachers need to attend professional development sessions in which they can learn about the tool and practice using it by watching video of teachers and students until they are able to gather data reliably. Additionally, the principal and the participating teacher need to get together to review the form to ensure that they agree on all the items on the form.

I suggest going through the observation tool line by line to ensure they will complete the form the same way. In some cases, this may include discussing how to address aspects of the class that are hard to see on video. For example, principal and teacher may need to come to consensus about how they will observe engagement. Before the end of this conversation, the principal should check to ensure that the collaborating teacher is completely confident about applying the evaluation tool to her class.

One option is for principal and teacher to go through the form and revise it based on the teacher's concerns. When teachers have real input into what is observed, they tend to be more receptive to the data. Also, since teachers work with students every day, there is a

---

[1]A copy of the 20-minute high-impact survey may be downloaded from the *High-Impact Instruction* companion website: http://www.corwin.com/highimpactinstruction/chapters/20-Minute_High-Impact_Survey.pdf

great chance that they have good insight into what data would be most helpful to consider.

Recording the Class. Once teacher and principal are confident that they both understand the observation tool, the principal should observe a lesson and video-record it. I suggest giving the participating teacher a choice about which class she would like to have observed, asking, "What class do you think you would learn the most from me observing?"

The principal can use whatever recording device is at hand. Frequently, that is an iPad, but any device that records the class and has reasonably good sound is acceptable. I suggest that the principal hold the camera and point it toward the teacher when the teacher is talking and point toward students when they are talking. The goal of video-recording the lesson is to get as much useful information as possible.

While recording the lesson, it is important to keep in mind the items on the evaluation form and ensure that the recording captures data that will enable the form to be completed. For example, if the form calls for an assessment of engagement, the principal might focus the camera on each student at the 10- and 20-minute point during the lesson. Of course, the principal will want to be as unobtrusive as possible.

The principal should record at least 20 minutes of a lesson and, if time permits, consider recording more—perhaps an entire 45-minute lesson. (The longer lessons that are typically used in block scheduling may be too long for many since it will take so long to watch the entire video.)

After the observation, the video is shared with the teacher. This may be done in many ways, including downloading a video from the recording device directly onto the collaborating teacher's computer, using a file-sharing site like Dropbox, using one of the commercial video-sharing sites mentioned in Chapter 2, or loading the video onto a jump drive or external drive and sharing the recording that way.

Watching and Evaluating the Lesson. Our research on coaching suggests that it is important that people have an opportunity to watch their video by themselves before discussing it with others. Otherwise, the conversation may be inhibited by the playing of the video and by the teacher's concerns about what the other person is thinking. A better plan, therefore, is for teacher and principal to watch the video separately and then come together to discuss what they saw.

While watching the video, both teacher and principal use the evaluation tool to focus their observation of the lesson. For example, a teacher using the 20-minute high-impact survey would look at student engagement, how time was used, type, kind, and level of question, ratio of positive to negative interactions, and all other items on the form.

The evaluation tool gives teacher and principal a shared perspective on what happened in the class and focuses their perception. However, the evaluation is not limited to that. When Tony Mosser sat down to view his lesson, he was interested in looking at engagement, but he discovered that the engagement was far higher than he expected. So, as his principal Bill Sommers explained to me, they ended up talking about something much different than they had planned.

> Tony planned to talk about student engagement, but the video showed students were very engaged, so we ended up talking about behavior management, especially about a couple of students who were roaming around the room. We talked about concepts of chemical and physical changes, and we got into several other discussions.

Meeting to Discuss the Video. Once teacher and principal have viewed the recording, they can get together to discuss their perspective on what happened. I suggest letting the teacher lead this conversation. The easiest way is simply to have the teacher talk about each item on the observation form. In *Unmistakable Impact* (2011), I list a number of questions that might help principals move through this discussion (see Figure 6.1).

Determining the Next Action. After principal and coach have discussed the observation, they should establish a next action. Productivity guru David Allen has written (2001) about the importance of clarifying exactly what you are going to do to bring about any form of improvement:

> In training and coaching thousands of professionals, I have found that lack of time is not the major issue for them (though they themselves may think it is); the real problem is a lack of clarity and definition about what a project really is, and what the associated next-action steps required are. (p. 19)

Some principals may want to use the questions coaches use. Also, principals may want to use the PEERS criteria to develop goals with coaches.

Teachers could be given the option to coach themselves or work with an instructional coach if one exists in the school.

Figure 6.1   Sample Questions

- Given the time we have today, what is the most important thing that you and I should be talking about? (Susan Scott)

- What if nothing changes? So what? What are the implications for you and your students? (Susan Scott)

- What is the ideal outcome? (Susan Scott)

- What can we do if we resolve this issue? (Susan Scott)

- Tell me about what you felt.

- Tell me a little bit about this...

- What leads you to believe...?

- What would we see and hear that would be evidence of this? (Bruce Wellman; Lucy West)

- What went well? What surprised you? What did you learn? What will you do differently next time?

- What do you think about what the students are doing here?

- On a scale from 1 to 10, how close are you to your ideal classroom? (Steve Barkley)

- What are you seeing that shows that the strategy is successful? (Steve Barkley)

- What impact would _____ have? (Steve Barkley)

- When have you seen _____? Can you make a connection between that time and this time? (Steve Barkley)

Why Video-Enhanced Teacher Evaluation Works

Video 6.1
Principals Using Video

www.corwin.com/ focusonteaching

Ensures Observations Are Reliable. One reason traditional teacher evaluations fail is that some teachers think principals didn't get it right when they observed a class; that is, that principals' observations are unreliable. In some cases, that is true—any human being's observations can be unreliable or incorrect. For example, the principal might not understand what an evaluation form asks her to see (for example, not understanding type, kind, and level of question) because she didn't receive sufficient training, because she is careless, or for some other reason. When teachers don't think their principals use evaluation forms correctly, they are less likely to learn from conversations with their principals about the evaluation.

As we have seen, when video-enhanced teacher evaluation is used, the process begins with the participating teacher and principal meeting to ensure they both understand the form being used. I suggest principals consider asking teachers if they want to modify the form to gather other data so that they have a voice in deciding what is being observed.

Ensuring that both teacher and principal have an accurate and shared understanding of the evaluation form goes a long way toward improving the evaluation conversation. Besides, if they disagree on what they saw, they can always go back to the video and check what the video reveals. Bill Sommers, principal and author, Minnetonka, Minnesota, says

> I'm going to suggest that in the high-stakes cultures in the urban centers, etc., where you have got to demonstrate certain competencies or whatever, you could throw that out with the teacher in the room a lot differently. Inter-rater reliability is always a problem. One principal comes in and evaluates a teacher and says, and I followed him—I am thinking of a guy in a middle school years ago, who said, "This is the worst teacher and we have got to get rid of him." I went in and said, "He is the most creative person I have ever seen." So, there is still that possibility, and with a video recording and having a conversation around it, I think there is going to be less of that.

Prevents Teacher Misconceptions About a Lesson. A second reason teachers and principals may not have a meaningful conversation about teacher evaluation is the reality, as I've noted throughout this book, that people don't know what it looks like when they do what they do. Even if a principal's observation is correct, the teacher may not believe it because he has a different understanding of what it looks like when he teaches. For example, a principal might accurately observe the ratio of interaction (a teacher's number of positive vs. corrective interactions) and tell the teacher that the ratio was 1:3. However, since she doesn't have a clear picture of how she teaches, the teacher might find this hard to believe and assume the principal got it wrong.

Teachers, like other professionals, don't have a clear picture of what it looks like when they teach. This means that when a principal and teacher get together to discuss a class, they are talking about two different things—what the principal observed and what the teacher observed.

> *I want to do more evaluations using video. I think it increases trust. I think it increases accuracy. You have the potential to deepen the conversations about instruction without focusing on "this is my opinion and this is what I saw. I don't care how it felt to you; this is what I saw."*
>
> —**Bill Sommers**, Author and Principal, Minnetonka, Minnesota

Using video solves this dilemma because the observation is based not on the principal and teacher's imperfect memory of the lesson but on the clear evidence of the video. In our experience, when a principal conducts an observation that doesn't involve video, he ends up spending a lot of time trying to convince the teacher that his view of reality is more correct than hers. When a principal uses video-enhanced professional learning, on the other hand, no convincing is required because the reality is right there on the film.

Allows Principals to Focus on the Class. One of the benefits of using video is that it releases observers from the need to take notes. As Winifred Gallagher (2009) explained in her book about attention, *Rapt: Attention and the Focused Life*, "science has determined that multitasking is for most practical purposes a myth, and that heeding its siren call leads to inefficiency and even danger." She goes on to say:

> You may think you're multitasking when you're listening to your boss's report while texting your lunch date, but what you're really doing is switching back and forth between activities. Despite your fond hopes, the extra effort involved actually makes you less rather than more productive; your

overall performance will be inefficient, error-prone, and more time-consuming than if you had done one thing at a time. As one attention expert ruefully observed after writing a book, "if your train of thought is interrupted even for a second, you have to go back and say, 'Where was I?' There are start-up costs each time as you reload everything into memory. Multi-tasking exacts a price, and people aren't as good at it as they think they are." (pp. 151–152)

When principals take notes during observations, they are forced, as Gallagher says, to "switch back and forth between activities," and this means that they inevitably miss important events when they're taking notes. Video-recording frees principals to focus their attention on teaching and complete the evaluation form later while watching the video. Further, once a lesson has been recorded, a principal can review the same event multiple times if he wishes to make sure he has gotten it right. In the words of principal and author Bill Sommers, "Writing takes me away from paying attention. If I have to write down notes, it splits my attention and you can only attend to one thing at a time. And, I can rest assured knowing that there is a backup for accuracy."

Captures More Than an Evaluation Form Can. Evaluation forms can gather a lot of important data, and they provide great data for setting goals and monitoring progress. But each classroom is a rich, complex environment, and no form can ever capture the full complexity of the classroom. Reading an evaluation form about a lesson is like reading the box scores after a ballgame. Sure, it gives you important data, but you see a lot more when you watch the game.

Using video allows you to see so much more about what happens during a lesson. Granted, recording ratios of interaction gives you valuable information, but seeing how a teacher shares positive information with students and how students respond to that praise shows you a lot more. Additionally, video often reveals important information that does not show up on a form. This was another aspect of video that Bill Sommers saw as helpful:

The other piece that was really nice about the video was that I could see how many students were engaged at the time, how they were responding to transitions, how they were responding to opportunities to share among themselves and give feedback. I could see all of those groups whereas from the teacher's spot, I am willing to choose my location in the room, the scan of my vision in terms of who am I making eye contact with at the specific moment as I am asking questions, or walking around, or specific interactions with students or a specific student at a time—that video gives you an entire encapsulation of what was going on. That was a real valuable piece. Otherwise you are limited to your physical being.

Makes Conversations More Collaborative, Reflective, and Real. For all the reasons mentioned, one of the problems with traditional conversations about teacher evaluation is that they often end up being arguments about different views of what happened in the classroom. Traditional teacher evaluation puts principals in the position of being experts, passing judgment on teachers. In some cases, the fact that principals are one up and teachers are one down leads to a conversation that looks more like a power struggle than a meaningful conversation. The principal tries to convince the teacher of his evaluation, and the teacher tries to explain why the observations miss the mark. Professionals don't want to be put in a one-down position (Schein, 2009), and consequently the conversation about an observation can turn into a meaningless power struggle. Video changes all of this.

Fostering Implementation

1. Walk the talk.
2. Shape culture.
3. Fight for resources.
4. Develop deep knowledge.
5. Employ partnership leadership.

Fostering Implementation

As seen, video-enhanced teacher evaluation is one way whereby principals can have a significant positive impact on professional learning in schools. Another way is by leading their schools in a manner that increases the likelihood that educators want to use video as a part of their professional learning. In the following, we will look at five strategies principals can use to accelerate implementation of video-enhanced professional development.

1. WALK THE TALK

The most high-impact strategy principals can use to encourage teachers to use video is probably also the simplest: Walk the talk. As President Kennedy said in 1960, "what we are speaks louder than what we say" (Senator Kennedy at Mormon Tabernacle, Salt Lake City, Utah, September 23, 1960). Principals can't expect teachers to courageously step up, take the risk, and learn from video if they are not willing to do the same. There are many ways for principals to "walk the talk."

People who choose to learn from video must be committed to learning, so principals who want their teachers to use video must first promote a learning culture. The easiest way to encourage others to be learners is simply to be a learner oneself. If we want students to be learners, teachers need to be learners, and if we want teachers to be learners, administrators need to be learners.

When principals are "first learners," they communicate what and how they are learning. To do this, they read books, articles, and blogs, watch videos, attend conferences, and so forth. Additionally, principals need to find ways to share their learning with the educators in their systems. This can be accomplished in many ways—by copying/sharing articles, buying books for staff, leading book study, sharing links to blogs and presentations, and so on.

Perhaps the most important way that leaders can encourage learning is to embody learning in their day-to-day actions. This means that leaders (a) listen with an intent to learn from others; (b) share ideas with humility and an openness to hearing others' thoughts about the ideas; and (c) show that they are reflecting on their actions and are open to seeing what data show about what they do and change based on what they learn. More than anything, it means that principals recognize the power of personal development and demonstrate a lust for learning.

Learning is a life force. When we learn, we grow and become more alive. But in many settings, learning is countercultural, with norms of behavior that encourage entropy rather than growth. In such cultures, learners have to demonstrate what can only be called deviant behavior: They have to stand up for learning, initially their own learning and then the learning of others, even though all around them the norm may be externalization of blame and resistance to change. If leaders want a learning culture in their schools, they have to be the first learners. To create learning cultures in which VPD can flourish, leaders have to embody the assumptions inherent in the culture they wish to create. As Mahatma Gandhi so famously stated, they need to "be the change they want to see."

2. SHAPE CULTURE

Edgar Schein (2010) in *Organizational Culture and Leadership* helps us understand what culture is and why leaders must be skillful culture shapers. I find Schein's work extremely helpful because he provides readers with a vocabulary for understanding culture and suggests how they can interpret and shape culture. For example, Schein writes that culture is manifest in "artifacts," "espoused values," and "assumptions."

Artifacts, according to Schein (2010), "at the surface level include all the phenomena that you would see, hear, and feel when you encounter a new group with an unfamiliar culture" (p. 23). In schools, artifacts might refer to newsletters, procedures for meetings, libraries of professional literature, blogs, methods for digital sharing of ideas, and so forth. Additionally, Schein writes,

> artifacts include the physical products of the group, such as the architecture of its physical environment; its language; its technology and products; its artistic creations; its style as embodied in clothing, manners of address, and emotional displays; its myths and stories told about the organization; its published list of values; and its observable rituals and ceremonies. (p. 23)

Leaders can shape culture by considering the artifacts that people in the school see, hear, and feel, and promote learning, especially learning with video, by putting artifacts in a school that reinforce the importance of learning and learning with video. For example, a school principal might use video-recording for her own professional growth so that others can see how video might be used successfully for other purposes. Additionally, principals could strive to get cameras in the hands of teachers and work with staff to develop procedures, such as those described in Chapters 4 and 5, to create psychologically safe environments. Principals can also shape culture by creating artifacts to promote learning by writing and sharing blogs, making journals and professional books widely available, and promoting the digital sharing of ideas.

I like to say that cultural artifacts, simply put, are what you see (a broader definition also includes what you hear and feel). Leaders who want to create a safe environment in which educators choose to learn from video can shape culture by considering what is seen within the walls and the digital environment of a school.

Schein (2010) writes that "the most important point to be made about this level of culture [artifacts] is that it is both easy to observe and very difficult to observe . . . It is especially dangerous to try to infer the deeper assumptions from artifacts alone because a person's interpretations will inevitably be projections of his or her own feelings and reactions" (p. 25). For this reason, when interpreting and shaping a culture that will support the use of video for professional learning, leaders also need to consider prevailing espoused values and assumptions.

Espoused values are statements people make about a culture. But as anyone who works in an organization knows, what people say is not always the same as what they do. As Schein (2010) writes, "In U.S. organizations, it is common to espouse *teamwork* while actually rewarding individual competitiveness" (p. 27). Further, espoused values can be too abstract or contradictory, "as when it [an organization] claims both highest quality and lowest cost" (p. 27).

Leaders in schools need to ensure that what they say about culture is indeed what is done. For example, if a school wants to create a psychologically safe environment for learning from video, team members need to learn nonjudgmental communication skills, teachers need to own their own video, the practice needs to be voluntary not compulsory, team members need to be chosen with care, and leaders need to choose their words carefully and take the time necessary to ensure that what is said is indeed what is done. In order for an espoused value to become a widely held underlying assumption, leaders, related to use of video, may have to frequently repeat that video is optional not mandatory and that video is owned by the teachers.

When a statement is said over and over and becomes an actual way of interacting or communicating, it may be taken for granted and, according to Schein (2010), "come to be treated as reality" (p. 27). This is what Schein refers to as basic assumptions. "Basic assumptions . . . [are] . . . are so taken for granted that you find little variation within a social unit . . . [When] a basic assumption comes to be strongly held in a group, members find behavior based on any other premise inconceivable" (p. 28). Schein goes on to say,

> Culture as a set of basic assumptions defines for us what to pay attention to, what things mean, how to react emotionally to what is going on, and what actions to take in various kinds of situations. After we have developed an integrated set of such assumptions . . . we will be maximally comfortable with others who share the same set of assumptions and very uncomfortable and vulnerable in situations where different assumptions operate because either we will not understand what is going on, or, worse, we will misperceive and misinterpret the actions of others. (p. 29)

What this all means is that talking about a cultural value is not enough. For example, involving staff in establishing norms for video learning teams can be powerful. But words that are not reflected in reality are fairly useless. Related to the use of video, leaders need to communicate in the school, district, and community that video is a power tool for professional learning and growth and ensure that those words are borne out in action.

Leaders can help translate values into assumptions by hiring for cultural values, but they also need to monitor teams to ensure that participants are treating each other with the openness and respect necessary for people to take the risk to learn from video. Sometimes a principal may even need to confront team members who are not acting in ways that are good for teacher learning and student growth.

I saw this in action at the University of Kansas Center for Research on Learning. I was a member of a group that met with a consultant who was helping us do some strategic planning related to research goals. Several times, it was very clear that one person was not embracing the process. He wasted a lot of everyone's time by confronting the facilitator. Eventually, the center director met with the team member one to one, explained that his behavior was slowing the team up, and offered to let him leave the team. He was gracious and respectful, but also clear and direct, and the team member changed his behavior after that 20-minute conversation.

I know about that conversation because I was the dysfunctional team member! The truth is that I had no idea that my behavior was such a problem; I just didn't get along with the facilitator. The director's empathetic but clear message woke me up to realizing what I was doing. From that meeting on, I was committed to making the process work. Of course, if I could have seen my behavior on video, my learning would have been even more powerful and faster.

3. FIGHT FOR RESOURCES

One of the most common things I hear leaders say is that they would like to have coaches, cameras for teachers, extra time for teachers to meet in video learning teams, or access to video-sharing sites, but they simply can't afford it. In many cases, although there is no doubt that schools could benefit from additional funding, the reality of funding is that some districts don't put professional learning at the top of the list. Why else would schools cut instructional coaches before they cut athletic coaches?

Principals who want their school to support video-enhanced learning need to fight for the resources their teachers need to implement VPD. Without adequate resources, many innovations will be dead in the water. For example, trying to implement team learning without providing time for it will almost certainly not succeed.

To implement VPD, a few relatively inexpensive items must be available. First, and most basically, teachers need cameras to record their class. During our interviews, we found that iPads were most commonly used for video recording. Regardless of what device is used, the most important thing is having cameras that are easy to use. (In Chapter 2, I present criteria for selecting cameras.)

One of the main barriers to implementing VPD is sharing video. Fortunately, many sites are surfacing (see the list on page 35 in Chapter 2) that make it easy to share confidential video. When people use a video-sharing site, they can record a class and then share it within the hour with their collaborating teacher.

Further, VLTs won't work unless the teams have time to meet. I remember once sitting in a team meeting during which the principal wanted teachers to collaborate in professional learning communities, so she asked teachers to add extra team meetings to their already busy day. Teachers decided to meet at 6:45 in the morning, but many were not at their best so early in the day. To them, rather than being a way of learning leading to productive collaboration, the meetings felt like a punishment.

Perhaps the most important resource principals ought to fight for is a full-time instructional coach in their school. Our research at the Kansas Coaching Project suggests that implementation of practices rarely happens without intensive professional support from a coach.

But hiring coaches is not enough. Coaches need professional development so that they can make a real difference by using video to set measurable goals with teachers, choosing teaching strategies, explaining and modeling those strategies, using video to monitor progress, and, ultimately, achieving the goals.

4. DEVELOP DEEP KNOWLEDGE

An often overlooked but critically important part of any instructional improvement process is principals' knowledge. If they are to lead any kind of professional development, principals need certain kinds of essential knowledge. For VPD, principals need to experience watching themselves on video and understand how vulnerable and how important it can be to watch yourself do work that is connected to your identity. But there is much more that principals need to know.

First, if a school is conducting professional learning, it always involves some kind of teaching practice. Whether a school adopts Marzano's *Art and Science of Teaching* (2007), Saphier's *The Skillful*

Teacher (2008), Randy Sprick's *CHAMPS* (2009), Wiggins and McTighe's *Understanding by Design* (2005), my *High-Impact Instruction* (2013), or any other approach or combination of approaches, naturally, the principal needs to have a deep understanding of those practices.

At the most basic level, principals need to know what practices have been adopted. To that end, I suggest schools create a one-page document that lists the practices being promoted. If there are too many practices to be listed on a single page, chances are there are too many practices for anyone to know in detail. As Michael Fullan so wisely put it in *Motion Leadership* (2010), "the more you know, the briefer you get" (p. 25).

Of course, simply knowing what practices are being promoted is not deep knowledge. Principals also need to fully understand what the practices are and how they are to be implemented. One way to accomplish that is through the use of checklists. Checklists take tacit knowledge and make it explicit, providing a document that can be used to confirm shared understanding.

Each item on the one-page list of practices may require two to four checklists. For example, teachers who are using learning maps might need separate checklists for describing a quality map, for the first day of the unit, for daily use, and for end-of-unit review. A principal who is promoting learning maps as one item on a list of practices should be able to describe clearly each item on each of the checklists. That is deep knowledge.

Additionally, principals who are conducting video-enhanced teacher evaluations need to fully understand each item on the evaluation form. All administrators in a system should be able to apply the evaluation criteria with a high degree of reliability. Few things are more frustrating for teachers than when administrators give them conflicting perspectives on walkthroughs or evaluations.

Finally, principals should understand how professional development procedures take place. For example, if their school is employing instructional coaching, principals should understand the components of coaching as they are described in Chapter 2 of this book or in some other coaching model. Similarly, if their school is implementing teams, principals should understand how learning teams (as described in Chapter 5) or professional learning communities are best organized. Finally, if their school is employing a school improvement process, and almost every school is, principals need to understand how that process can lead teachers to understand, agree with, and commit to a plan.

5. EMPLOY PARTNERSHIP LEADERSHIP

Ultimately, principals' support for implementation of VPD hinges on their ability to lead. Although leadership is a much talked-about but often little-understood concept, certain tactics can help principals create the conditions necessary for VPD to thrive and succeed.

Relationship Building. According to emotional intelligence expert Daniel Goleman and colleagues (2002), "roughly 50 to 70 percent of how employees perceive their organization's climate can be traced to the actions of one person: the leader" (p. 18). In other chapters in this book (especially Chapter 5), I have written about communication skills that leaders can employ to increase their emotional intelligence. Effective communicators find common ground with others (Knight, 2011), build emotional connections (Gottman, 2002), redirect conversations away from unhealthy interactions such as gossip, control emotions, and truly listen (Scott, 2002).

Perhaps the most important relationship-building strategy or approach is for leaders to have faith in their teachers. "Faith" in other people, Paul Freire (1970) wrote, "is an a priori requirement for dialogue; the 'dialogical [person]' believes in other [people] even before [meeting] them face to face" (p. 90). Just as an excellent teacher sees potential in his students, an excellent leader expects excellence in her staff. According to Henry Cloud (2009), "connection happens when one person has a true emotional investment in the other, and the other person experiences that and it is returned. To do that requires that the character gets out of oneself long enough to know, experience, and value the other" (p. 57).

Integrity. "Leadership," according to General Norman Schwartzkopf, "is a potent combination of strategy and character. But if you must be without one, be without strategy." A leader who has vision, empathy, and knowledge but lacks integrity is a leader who may struggle to succeed. Integrity involves several attributes, including honesty, reliability, and respect for others.

In *Respect: An Exploration* (2000), Sarah Lawrence-Lightfoot notes that "respect is commonly seen as deference to status and hierarchy; as driven by duty, honor, and a desire to avoid punishment, shame or embarrassment" (p. 9). At the same time, however, she presents portraits of leaders who are "the powerful persons in . . .

relationships . . . those usually seen on the receiving end of respect," . . . leaders who "each believe that it is impossible to do the work that they do without offering respect, creating a relationship with respect at the center" (p. 10).

There are no simple strategies for what Lawrence-Lightfoot calls "creating relationships with respect at the center," but leaders who fail to show respect for others will struggle to succeed. At its heart, authentic respect may be described as never failing to see people as complete human beings. Not as objects to be moved around, but as people whose voices matter and who should be heard. Robert Sutton (2010) has written, "I've never met a boss who wants to leave people feeling demeaned, disrespected, and de-energized. Yet many bosses are buffeted by forces that bring out insensitivity and nastiness" (p. 220). Effective leaders always treat others with humanity and respect.

Balance. Despite our best efforts to do otherwise, our work life becomes a part of our home, and our home life, in turn, affects our work. Many have spoken persuasively about keeping the two worlds separate, but in my experience, that's much easier said than done. If we are worried about a family member's health, for example, it is difficult not to be affected by that worry on the job. And if things are highly stressful at work, it is difficult not to bring some of it home. The opposite, of course, is also true. When we experience joyful events at home or at work (say, a newborn baby or a student success story), whether consciously or not, those experiences can lift up everyone around us.

Being a principal can dramatically interfere with our ability to be fathers, mothers, and significant others to our partners in life. To change the future one day at a time, one child at a time, requires tremendous energy and commitment. If we are not careful, we may find ourselves spending too much time at work. Like other potentially addictive substances, such as alcohol, work held in moderation is fine, but when work becomes our only reality, it's time to change.

Our lives outside of school are truly just as important as our lives inside schools. We all, teachers, principals, researchers, need to be vigilant in making sure that a blind focus on one life doesn't end the other. Our students need committed, passionate educators. But our families need us, too. We need to keep them at the heart of our lives. In truth, chances are we never will achieve our professional goals if we try to do them on our own anyway.

Turning Ideas Into Action

STUDENTS

The very people who have all the experience receiving teaching—students—are seldom asked about what kind of instruction and learning help them. Students will never have the final say on defining good teaching, but asking students for their opinion on what kind of instruction and learning experiences help them learn can be very informative.

One way to do this is to video-record students talking about their learning or circulate surveys for students to complete. Then staff and administrators can get together to discuss evaluation tools.

TEACHERS

Evaluation tools won't have much impact unless teachers understand them and agree that they are appropriate and meaningful. For that reason, teachers should have sufficient professional development to completely understand evaluation frameworks. Additionally, teachers should have the opportunity to talk about aspects of an evaluation framework that they don't understand or that they think is misguided. Evaluation should be seen as a tool for growth, not a form of top-down pressure. Involving teachers in discussing and even co-creating an evaluation form can increase the likelihood that they will see evaluation frameworks as tools for growth and development rather than tools for compliance and control.

COACHES

We suggest that to protect the coaching relationship, coaches do not perform evaluations. In part, this is because many coaches are not certified supervisors and, therefore, lack sufficient training to conduct evaluations or hold follow-up debriefs about evaluations. More important, however, it is because there is a strong possibility that their evaluative role will damage their coaching relationship. Coaching is a peer-to-peer conversation, one teacher talking to another. When we are evaluated by somebody, that person assumes a supervisory role and thereby changes the peer-to-peer nature of the relationship. And the reality is that many people don't speak with their supervisors as openly as they do with their peers, primarily since they don't want their supervisors to give them a poor evaluation.

Nevertheless, coaches do have an essential role in video-enhanced teacher evaluation. Once a teacher has completed his

(Continued)

(Continued)

conversation with his principal and set a goal, the coach can partner with the collaborating teacher to assist him in trying to meet goals. Indeed, goal setting that doesn't include follow-up such as coaching seldom leads to real, meaningful change that improves learning for students.

PRINCIPALS

The most important thing principals can do to promote learning is to use video for their own professional growth and then communicate to their staff what they are learning from doing it. Additionally, when principals use video as a part of teacher evaluation, they must have a complete and correct understanding of the evaluation framework.

SYSTEM LEADERS AND POLICY MAKERS

First, leaders must select an evaluation framework that works for their system. One way to ensure that the right assessment tool is selected is to involve teachers in choosing a method of evaluation that they see as most useful. Once a framework is selected, leaders must ensure that everyone who uses it, administrators and teachers, has a complete and correct understanding of how the assessment tool is used. Using an assessment tool incorrectly, as happens all too often, is worse than no assessment at all, as it damages trust and decreases morale.

Second, leaders and policy makers must ensure that principals receive the professional development they need to develop the deep knowledge necessary to lead professional development. Thus, they need to attend workshops, receive coaching, and practice in classrooms to ensure that they understand the practices and evaluation system in place.

Perhaps the most important thing leaders can do to support principals is to free up time for them to do the work that most principals want to do: be instructional leaders. To that end, system leaders need to ensure that principals are not forced into activities that have no impact on student learning, such as conducting evaluations that have no impact on teacher practice and learning, and they need to think carefully about what meetings principals are required to attend. For example, elementary principals shouldn't be required to attend meetings that apply only to secondary principals and vice versa. Also, if a message can be handled by e-mail rather than in a face-to-face meeting, that's usually a better option because it saves time. Generally, every effort should be made to provide principals with more time to focus on actions that promote student learning.

TO SUM UP

Principals play an essential part in ensuring that video is introduced into schools successfully. To foster widespread productive use of video, principals play two essential roles: (a) making video an optional part of teacher evaluation and (b) creating settings in which teachers, coaches, and teams can successfully implement VPD.

To make video an optional part of teacher evaluation, principals can

- Meet with teachers to explain the observation form
- Observe and video-record a lesson
- Watch the video and complete the evaluation
- Prompt the collaborating teacher to watch the video and complete the evaluation
- Meet with the teacher to discuss what they both found using the evaluation form to analyze the video
- Set goals for instructional improvement, perhaps by employing the PEERS approach to goal setting

To create a setting in which educators can successfully implement VPD, principals can

- Walk the talk by using video to promote their own professional growth
- Shape culture by creating artifacts that reflect a culture of safety and learning, involving everyone in developing norms that promote safety and learning, and intervening when necessary to ensure that what is said about a culture is reflected in how people act
- Fight for resources so that teachers get the technology, collaboration time, and support, especially coaching, necessary to enable them to implement VPD
- Build relationships
- Avoid dehumanizing practices

GOING DEEPER

There are many approaches to teacher evaluation and assessment. At the time of this writing, the two most popular are Charlotte Danielson's *Enhancing Professional Practice: A Framework for Teaching* (2007) and Robert Marzano's Evaluation Model (www.marzanoevaluation. com). Many systems are also using the 20-minute high-impact survey from my *High-Impact Instruction* (2013).

Edgar Schein's *Organizational Culture and Leadership* (2010) is the seminal work on assessment, and if you are interested in understanding and leading culture, you will benefit greatly from this book.

Henry Cloud's *Integrity: The Courage to Meet the Demands of Reality* (2009) provides strategies that can help anyone approach work and life with integrity. Robert Sutton's *Good Boss, Bad Boss: How to Be the Best and Learn From the Worst* (2010) is maybe the best leadership book I've read about the ways power corrupts and how leaders can fight to not let it happen.

Sarah Lawrence-Lightfoot's *Respect* (2000) portrays five leaders— a nurse-midwife, a pediatrician, a teacher, an artist, and a professor— who all make respect a central part of their practice. Finally, Stewart D. Friedman's *Total Leadership: Be a Better Leader, Have a Richer Life* (2008) explains why we should strive for balance in our lives and how we can make it a reality rather than just a dream.

REFERENCES
AND FURTHER READINGS

Allen, D. (2001). *Getting things done: The art of stress-free productivity.* New York, NY: Penguin Books Ltd.

Amabile, T., & Kramer, S. (2011). *The progress principle: Using small wins to ignite joy, engagement, and creativity at work.* Boston, MA: Harvard Business School Publishing.

Archer, A. L., & Hughes, C. (2011). *Explicit instruction: Effective and efficient teaching.* New York, NY: Guilford Press.

Barkley, S. G. (2010). *Quality teaching in a culture of coaching.* Lanham, MD: Rowman & Littlefield.

Bate, W. J. (1979). *John Keats.* Cambridge, MA: Belknap Press of Harvard University Press.

Block, P. (1993). *Stewardship: Choosing service over self-interest.* San Francisco, CA: Berrett-Koehler.

Bloom, B. S. (Ed.). (1956). *Taxonomy of educational objectives, handbook 1: Cognitive domain.* White Plains, NY: Longman.

Bloom, G. S., Castagna, C. L., Moir, E., & Warren, B. (2005). *Blended coaching: Skills and strategies to support principal development.* Thousand Oaks, CA: Corwin.

Bohm, D. (1996). *On dialogue.* New York, NY: Routledge.

Bossidy, L., & Charan, R. (2004). *Confronting reality: Doing what matters to get things right.* New York, NY: Random.

Bradley, B., Knight, J., Harvey, S., Hock, M., Knight, D., Skrtic, T., Brasseur-Hock, I., & Deshler, D. D. (2013). Improving instructional coaching to support middle school teachers in the United States. In T. Plomp & N. Nieveen (Eds.), *Educational design research—Part B: Introduction and illustrative cases* (pp. 299–318). Enschede, the Netherlands: SLO. http://international.slo.nl/publications/edr/contents/c15/

Bryk, A. A., & Schneider, B. L. (2002). *Trust in schools: A core resource for improvement.* New York, NY: Russell Sage Foundation.

Bulgren, J., Schumaker, J., & Deshler, D. D. (1993). *The concept mastery routine.* Lawrence, KS: Edge Enterprises.

Burkin, J. M. (2009). *Practical literacy coaching: A collection of tools to support your work.* Thousand Oaks, CA: Corwin.

Christensen, C. (1997). *The innovator's dilemma: The revolutionary book that will change the way you do business.* New York, NY: Harper Collins.

Christensen, C., Curtis, C. W., & Horn, M. B. (2008). *Disrupting class: How disruptive innovation will change the way the world learns.* New York, NY: McGraw Hill.

City, E. A., Elmore, R. F., Fiarman, S. E., & Teitel, L. (2009). *Instruction rounds in education: A network approach to improving teaching and learning.* Boston, MA: Harvard Education Press.

Cloud, H. (2009). *Integrity: The courage to meet the demands of reality.* New York, NY: HarperCollins.

Cloud, H., & Townsend, J. (2004). *Boundaries: When to say yes, when to say no—To take control of your life.* Grand Rapids, MI: Zondervan Publishing House.

Costa, A., & Garmston, R. (2002). *Cognitive coaching: A foundation for renaissance schools* (2nd ed.). Norwood, MA: Christopher-Gordon Publishers.

Danielson, C. (2007). *Enhancing professional practice: A framework for teaching.* Alexandria, VA: Association for Supervision and Curriculum Development.

Davenport, T. H. (2005). *Thinking for a living: How to get better performance and results from knowledge workers.* Boston, MA: Harvard Business School.

Doran, G. T. (1981). There's a S.M.A.R.T. way to write management's goals and objectives. *Management Review, 70*(11), 35–36.

DuFour, R., & Eaker, R. E. (1998). *Professional learning communities at work: Best practices for enhancing student achievement.* Bloomington, IN: National Education Service.

DuFour, R., & Fullan, M. (2013). *Cultures built to last: Systemic PLCs at work.* Bloomington, IN: Solution Tree Press.

Dweck, C. S. (2007). *Mindset: The new psychology of success.* New York, NY: Random House.

Edmondson, A. (2012). *Teaming: How organizations learn, innovate, and compete in the knowledge economy.* San Francisco, CA: Jossey Bass.

Ellis, E., Deshler, D. D., Lenz, B. K., Schumaker, J. B., & Clark, F. (1991). An instructional model for teaching learning strategies. *Focus on Exceptional Children, 23*(6), 1–24.

Fisher, R., & Brown, S. (1989). *Getting together: Building relationships as we negotiate.* New York, NY: Penguin.

Fisher, R., & Shapiro, D. (2006). *Beyond reason: Using emotions as you negotiate.* New York, NY: Penguin Group.

Fredrickson, B. (2009). *Positivity: Top-notch research reveals the 3 to 1 ratio that will change your life.* New York, NY: Three River Press.

Freire, P. (1970). *Pedagogy of the oppressed.* New York, NY: Continuum.

Friedman, S. (2008). *Total leadership: Be a better leader, have a richer life.* Boston, MA: Harvard Business School Publishing.

Fritz, R. (1984). *The path of least resistance: Learning to become the creative force in your own life.* New York, NY: Ballantine Books.

Fullan, M. (2001). *The meaning of educational change* (3rd ed.). New York, NY: Penguin Group.

Fullan, M. (2008). *The six secrets of change: What the best leaders do to help their organizations survive and thrive.* San Francisco, CA: Jossey-Bass.

Fullan, M. (2010). *Motion leadership: The skinny on becoming change savvy.* Thousand Oaks, CA: Corwin.

Gallagher, W. (2009). *Rapt: Attention and the focused life.* New York, NY: Penguin Group.

Gallwey, T. (1974). *The inner game of tennis.* New York, NY: Random House.

Gardner, D. P., & Larsen, Y. W. (1983). *A nation at risk: The imperative for educational reform.* Washington, DC: Members of the National Commission on Excellence in Education.

Gawande, A. (2011). *The checklist manifesto: How to get things right.* New York, NY: Metropolitan.

Goleman, D. (1995). *Emotional intelligence: Why it can matter more than IQ.* New York, NY: Bantam Dell.

Goleman, D., Boyatzis, R., & McKee, A. (2002). *Primal leadership: Realizing the power of emotional intelligence.* Boston, MA: Harvard Business School Press.

Gottman, J. (2002). *The relationship cure: A 5-step guide to strengthening your marriage, family and friendships.* New York, NY: Three Rivers Press.

Gottman, J. M., & Silver, N. (1999). *The seven principles for making marriage work.* New York, NY: Crown.

Greenleaf, R. K. (2002). *Servant leadership: A journey into the nature of legitimate power and greatness, 25th anniversary edition.* Mahwah, NJ: Paulist Press.

Grenny, J., Patterson, K., Maxfield, D., & McMillan, R. (2013). *Influencer: The new science of leading change* (2nd ed.). New York, NY: McGraw-Hill.

Halvorson, H. (2011). *9 things successful people do differently.* Watertown, MA: Harvard Business Review Press.

Hattie, H. (2008). *Visible learning: A synthesis of over 800 meta-analyses relating to achievement.* New York, NY: Routledge.

Hattie, J. (2011). *Visible learning for teachers: Maximizing. impact on learning.* New York, NY: Routledge.

Heath, C., & Heath, D. (2010). *Switch: How to change things when change is hard.* New York, NY: Random House.

Heath, C., & Heath, D. (2013). *Decisive: How to make better choices in life and work.* New York, NY: Random House.

Heifetz, R. A., & Linsky, M. (2002). *Leadership on the line: Staying alive through the dangers of leading.* Boston, MA: Harvard Business School Press.

Hemingway, E. (1926). *The sun also rises.* New York, NY: Scribner.

Hock, M., Schumaker, J., & Deshler, D. D. (2001). The case for strategic tutoring. *Educational Leadership, 58*(7), 50–52.

Hollingsworth, J., & Ybarra, S. (2008). *Explicit direct instruction: The power of the well-crafted, well-taught lesson.* Thousand Oaks, CA: Corwin.

Isaacs, E. (1999). *Dialogue and the art of thinking together.* New York, NY: Doubleday.

Kauchak, D. P., & Eggen, P. D. (2005). *Introduction to teaching: Becoming a professional.* Upper Saddle River, NJ: Merrill Prentice Hall.

Kegan, R., & Lahey, L. (2001). *How the way we talk can change the way we learn.* San Francisco, CA: Jossey-Bass.

Killion, J., & Harrison, C. (2006). *Taking the lead: New roles for teachers and school-based coaches.* Oxford, OH: Learning Forward.

Killion, J., & Todnem, G. R. (1991). A process of personal theory building. *Educational Leadership, 48*(2), 14–16.

Knight, J. (2007). *Instruction coaching: A partnership approach to improving instruction.* Thousand Oaks, CA: Corwin.

Knight, J. (Ed.). (2008). *Coaching: Approaches and perspectives.* Thousand Oaks, CA: Corwin.

Knight, J. (2011). *Unmistakable impact: A partnership approach for dramatically improving instruction.* Thousand Oaks, CA: Corwin.

Knight, J. (2013). *High impact instruction: A framework for great teaching.* Thousand Oaks, CA: Corwin.

Kise, J. A. G. (2006). *Differentiated coaching: A framework for helping teachers change.* Thousand Oaks, CA: Corwin.

Lawrence-Lightfoot, S. (2000). *Respect: An exploration.* Cambridge, MA: Perseus Books.

Lemov, D. (2010). *Teach like a champion: 49 techniques that put students on the path to college.* San Francisco, CA: Jossey-Bass.

Liu, E. (2004). *Guiding lights: How to mentor—and find life's purpose.* New York, NY: Ballantine Books.

Lopez, S. (2013). *Making hope happen: Create the future you want for yourself and others.* New York, NY: Atria Books.

Love, N. (2009). *Using data to improve learning for all: A collaborative inquiry approach.* Thousand Oaks, CA: Corwin.

MacDonald, E. (2013). *The skillful team leader: A resource for overcoming hurdles to professional learning for student achievement.* Thousand Oaks, CA: Corwin.

Marzano, R. (2007). *The art and science of teaching: A comprehensive framework for effective instruction.* Alexandria, VA: Association for Supervision and Curriculum Development.

Moran, M. C. (2007). *Differentiated literacy coaching: Scaffolding for student and teacher success.* Alexandria, VA: Association for Supervision and Curriculum Development.

Palmer, P. J. (1998). *The courage to teach: Exploring the inner landscape of a teacher's life.* San Francisco, CA: Jossey-Bass.

Palmer, P. J. (2004). *A hidden wholeness: The journey toward an undivided life.* San Francisco, CA: Jossey-Bass.

Palmer, P. J. (2007). *The courage to teach: Exploring the inner landscape of a teacher's life* (10th ed.). San Francisco, CA: Jossey-Bass.

Patterson, K., Grenny, J., Maxfield, D., McMillan, R., & Switzler, A. (2008). *Influencer: The power to change anything.* New York, NY: McGraw-Hill.

Patterson, K., Grenny, J., Maxfield, D., McMillan, R., & Switzler, A. (2013). *Influencer: The power to change anything* (2nd ed.). New York, NY: McGraw-Hill.

Popham, W. J. (2013). *Evaluating America's teachers: Mission possible?* Thousand Oaks, CA: Corwin.

Prochaska, J. O., Norcross, J. C., & DiClemente, C. C. (1994). *Changing for good: A revolutionary six-stage program for overcoming bad habits and moving your life positively forward.* New York, NY: Avon Books.

Reinke, W., Herman, K., & Sprick, R. (2011). *Motivational interviewing for effective classroom management: The classroom check-up.* New York, NY: Guilford Press.

Rifkin, J. (2009). *The empathic civilization: The race to global consciousness in a world crisis.* New York, NY: Penguin Group.

Roehler, L. R., & Duffy, G. G. (1984). Direct explanation of comprehension processes. In G. G. Duffy, L. R. Saphier, J., Haley-Speca, M., & Gower, R. (2008). *The skillful teacher: Building your teaching skills.* Acton, MA: Research for Better Teaching.

Roehler, L. R., & J. Mason (Eds.). *Comprehension instruction: Perspectives and suggestions* (pp. 265–280). New York, NY: Longman.

Schein, E. H. (2009). *Helping: How to offer, give, and receive help.* San Francisco, CA: Berrett-Koehler.

Schein, E. H. (2010). *Organizational culture and leadership.* San Francisco, CA: Jossey-Bass.

Schlechty. P. (2011). *Engaging students: The next level of working on work.* San Francisco, CA: Jossey-Bass.

Schön, D. (1991). *The reflective practitioner: How professionals think in action.* New York, NY: Perseus.

Scott, S. (2002). *Fierce conversations: Achieving success at work and in life, one conversation at a time.* New York, NY: Berkley Publishing Group.

Seligman, M. (2011). *Flourish: A visionary new understanding of happiness and well-being.* New York, NY: Simon & Schuster.

Senge, P. (2006). *The fifth discipline: The art and practice of the learning organization.* London: Random House.

Sprick, R. S. (2009). *CHAMPS: A proactive and positive approach to classroom management* (2nd ed.). Eugene, OR: Pacific Northwest Press.

Sprick, R. S., Knight, J., Reinke, W., Skyles, T., & Barnes, I. (2010). *Coaching classroom management: Strategies and tools for administrators and coaches* (2nd ed.) with DVD. Eugene, OR: Pacific Northwest Press.

Stone, D., Patton, B., & Heen, S. (1999). *Difficult conversations: How to discuss what matters most.* New York, NY: Penguin.

Sutton, R. I. (2010). *Good boss, bad boss: How to be the best and learn from the worst.* New York, NY: Hachette Book Group.

Tedlow, R. (2010). *Denial: Why business leaders fail to look facts in the face—and what to do about it.* New York, NY: Penguin Group.

Troen, V., & Boles, K. (2014). *The power of teacher rounds: A guide for facilitators, principals, and department chairs.* Thousand Oaks, CA: Corwin.

Tschannen-Moran, B., & Tschannen-Moran, M. (2010). *Evocative coaching: Transforming our schools one conversation at a time.* San Francisco, CA: Jossey-Bass.

U.S. Department of the Army. (2004). *The U.S. Army leadership field manual: Battle-tested wisdom for leaders in an organization.* Washington, DC: Headquarters, Dept. of the Army.

Wellman, B. (2004). *Data-driven dialogue: A facilitator's guide to collaborative inquiry.* Sherman, CT: Mitra Via, LLC.

West, L., & Staub, F. (2003). *Content-focused coaching: Transforming mathematics lessons.* Norwood, MA: Christopher-Gordon Publishers.

Wheatley, M. (2002). *Turning to one another: Simple conversations to restore hope to the future.* San Francisco, CA: Berrett-Koehler.

Wheatley, M. (2009). *Turning to one another: Simple conversations to restore hope to the future* (2nd ed.). San Francisco, CA: Berrett-Koehler.

Wiggins, G., & McTighe, J. (2005). *Understanding by design.* Alexandria, VA: Association for Supervision and Curriculum Development.

INDEX

CORWIN
A SAGE Company

The Corwin logo—a raven striding across an open book—represents the union of courage and learning. Corwin is committed to improving education for all learners by publishing books and other professional development resources for those serving the field of PreK–12 education. By providing practical, hands-on materials, Corwin continues to carry out the promise of its motto: **"Helping Educators Do Their Work Better."**

Advancing professional learning for student success

Learning Forward (formerly National Staff Development Council) is an international association of learning educators committed to one purpose in K–12 education: Every educator engages in effective professional learning every day so every student achieves.